THE INTIMATE MIND

THE INTIMATE MIND

Illuminating Emotion and Transformation

Tempa Dukte Lama

Olmo Ling
Pittsburgh 2011

Olmo Ling Publications
1101 Greenfield Avenue
Pittsburgh, PA 15217
www.olmoling.org

Printed in the United States of America.

This edition printed on acid-free paper.

Library of Congress Control Number: 2011927655

ISBN 13: 978-0-9835-4560-6
ISBN 10: 0-9835-4560-X

Designed and typeset by James P. Brommer in 10/16 Sabon.

Dedicated to my

MOTHER and FATHER

CONTENTS

FOREWORD

It is with great pleasure that I am able to introduce Tempa Dukte Lama's book, *The Intimate Mind*. In 1983, when he was a little boy of six, Tempa Dukte was presented to the monastery by his parents. He grew up with me and brought happiness to our community with his art and creativity. After eight years of schooling here, he continued his education at St. Luke's Missionary School and had further education at Punjab University Chandigarh, India. Now Tempa Dukte presides over Olmo Ling, a Bön teaching center in the American city of Pittsburgh, Pennsylvania.

Millions of people have spent millions of hours in study, practice, and meditation in order to cultivate the ultimate state of awakening that has no words to describe it. While much has been written about how to reach this place of primordial purity, it is only in our mastery of aspiration and intent that we are able to stay on the path toward the realization of our true nature. Dominating this sense of purpose must be the indispensable quality of compassion, which makes full use of good hearts and kind intentions. After all, the very purpose of one's activity is to become someone who can enable others to become Buddhas themselves. One has to find the capacity and energy in one's self to do this. One must have the firm intention to understand, purify, and perfect oneself so that one can aid all other beings to become Buddhas.

Through his own skillful means, Tempa Dukte has given us *The Intimate Mind* as a guide to help those on the path of awakening to understand that intimacy means allowing for the possibility to become one with the object we engage with, and that in that oneness there are no possibilities for distraction, attachment, chaos, fear, or judgment. That is where compassion resides, and it is only through compassion that liberation for oneself and others becomes possible. Tempa uses the term "Intimate Mind" to describe this relationship and to help us understand how to follow the path of a compassionate being. May we all attain liberation into our true nature!

Menri Trizin 33rd
Spiritual Head of Bön
Dolanji, India
January, 2009

THE INTIMATE MIND

Through the unsurpassed potential of all wisdom beings
and the blessings of all great teachers
may we not cling to the objects of sensual distraction
so that we can enjoy the treasury of contentment.
By not grasping the illusory appearances of phenomena as real
may we realize their lack of inherent nature.
By not giving rise to desire-attachment
may all beings realize the treasury of innate wisdom.
Clearing the obstruction of delusive conditioning
may we gain trust of confidence in the nature of our own mind.
Not letting concepts and mere words carry us away
may we experience the true meaning of reality.
Not remaining bound by relative appearances
may we enable the causes of our suffering
to self-liberate into their true nature.
Having met with the path of skillful means and recognized its preciousness
may we gain the wisdom of cognition.
Within the spontaneous manifestation of clarity
as the unification of awareness and emptiness
may we recognize our true nature.
By dissolving all causes and conditioning of affliction
may we abide within the true nature of our mind.
May we generate true love and compassion
so that all beings can benefit.
By clearing all obscurations of body, speech, and mind
may all beings be free from suffering and attain liberation.
May all my above aspirational wishes
come true in the form of great prayers and dedication.

PART I

THE THOUGHT THAT TURNS THE MIND
TOWARD ITS ESSENCE

May all sentient beings water
the causal seeds of happiness.
May all sentient beings clear
the causal seeds of suffering.
May all sentient beings be free from the duality
of both happiness and suffering.
May all sentient beings
always be in touch
with the Intimate Mind of immeasurable equanimity.

CHAPTER 1

INTRODUCTION

The Intimate Mind is the mind in its natural state. It is pure, clear, and stable. Primordial. It is free from the grasp of delusive ignorance. It has the strength to distinguish between the wholesome and unwholesome nature of our conditioning and our habits. The Intimate Mind is our capacity to perceive things as they are.

When we perceive an object, we sometimes reveal our own fear, anger, hatred, jealousy, or envy. We may believe that the object itself is the cause of our feelings, the cause of our misery or unhappiness. But the same objects that we regard as the cause of our misery, can, in a different moment, serve as the cause of our happiness, joy, and inspiration.

If this is the case, how can the Intimate Mind help us see clearly? The Intimate Mind is the capacity of our mind to be equanimous—calm and poised. That capacity can keep us strong, stable, and clear so that we can provide space to ourselves, to others, or to objects that we are encountering, so that they can manifest according to their own nature. The intimate nature of our mind makes us stable so that we are not easily carried away by external objects. The Intimate Mind does not allow the mind to overwhelm the object with our conditioning (whether that projection is expressed as a projection, as speculation, or as judgment). The Intimate Mind allows us to approach whatever we encounter with positive thoughts. It is the capacity of the mind that always enables us to reach out to others and to reach inward to ourselves with genuine feelings of love, compassion, and care.

We call this the Intimate Mind because we are, without fear, being intimate with our feelings, with the state of our being, with the functioning of our stream of consciousness, and with the object of our mind. When we are intimate, we can become one with the object that we are intimate with, leaving no space for chaos, no space for distraction, no space for the unnecessary arousal of judgment, fear, or any of the emotions that cause suffering and separation. The Intimate Mind is an expression of what we become as we travel the path of compassionate beings.

How do we cultivate the heart and mind of a compassionate being? And how do we follow this path of practice in the journey of living life? We are all very fortunate to already have this heart, this mind, and the possibility of their union. We plant the causal seed of awakening when we unify our heart and mind—wisdom and compassion—through the medium of wholesome intention. Sometimes our heart is open, but our mind is not ready to accept it or may even turn away from it. At other times our mind tries to understand but our heart is not ready to accept. When heart and mind disagree, we feel emotional stress and pain. If we bring heart and mind together, we end the unnecessary stress that we experience in our lives because of their separation.

The unification of wisdom and compassion is the potential to awaken that is inherent in all of us. By nature, we all have the potential to awaken and we all can become compassionate beings. This inherent potential is called the Buddhahood of base. Under the strong influence of ignorance and afflictive conditioning such as attachment, greed, hatred, anger, judgment, and fear, we distance ourselves from this potential. The way through which we reconnect with our innate potential and actualize the causal seed of awakening is called the Buddhahood of path. The initiative force for this path is our development of a wholesome thought or intention. This wholesome intention binds our heart and mind together in the nature of oneness and begins to unfold the nurturing qualities of the Intimate Mind. With the gift of a unified heart and mind, everything is possible. The realization that we attain through following this path is the Buddhahood of fruit. When we attain the Buddhahood of fruit, we actualize our true nature of intrinsic purity. To become a Buddha, we eliminate all conditioning that afflicts our stream of consciousness. The mind of a Buddha is purified of all negative emotions and free from the obscuration of intellect.

We need all three, the Buddhahood of base, path, and fruit, in order to actualize and attain the fruit. Without the base, there can be no path. Without the path and the base, there can be no fruit. By learning about and practicing the Buddhahood of path and coming to experience the Buddhahood of fruit, we expand and strengthen our motivation and make it more unconditional. This is because our practice gives us insight into the elements in our mind that obstruct our potential and the elements that strengthen it. The path of a compassionate being is, in essence, about this motivation.

I wrote this book because this practice helped me. It is my

hope that this book will offer you a view from which to see your situation and life. If you look into what is making you unhappy and what is making you happy, if you can recognize the causes and conditions of your situation and your state of being, you will be able to move further along the path of the compassionate being.

CHAPTER 2

THE WAY OF THE INTIMATE MIND

When the wonders of the mind
abide in the open heart,
the Intimate Mind shines forth.

This is the essence of awakening: our mind and heart are one.
Their oneness is the unification of wisdom and compassion. This
unification makes us what we truly are. The mind that is not separate from the heart is the Intimate Mind. The very basic teachings
of Bön and Buddhism allow us to feel our true nature by unifying
our heart and mind. These teachings offer a simple and powerful practice of basic humanness: compassion, love, joy, and equanimity. These four qualities are interdependent. They can only be
complete when all four are present as one. They need each other.

The intention to help others develops the openness of our
heart and our capacity to see we are not separate from others.

Compassion is the main medium, the seed that gives birth to the new plant that is love. When you are in a state of love, your mental, emotional, and physical experience is one of eternal joy. Your whole being feels relaxed, at ease and filled with joy. We may wish we could stay in this state forever. Yet, this is not what happens. Under the influence of ignorance, the mind tries to hold on to the experience of a blissful state of our being. This creates suffering. The nature of the Intimate Mind, on the other hand, allows us to let things be as they are. It increases our capacity of wisdom to understand the nature of impermanence, that things and feelings do not stay the same forever. To me, it is not important whether a joyful state of our being stays for long or short periods of time. What is important is to become familiar with the process that generates the eternal joy within us and the process of its dissolution. This familiarity is awareness. Awareness is important on the path of compassionate beings; it enables us to let go.

QUALITIES OF THE INTIMATE MIND

The four essential qualities of compassion, love, joy, and equanimity are the basic inherent qualities of the awakened mind. If one of them is missing, we are not fully realized. To be completely awake, we have to surpass our obscurations. We have to go beyond the obscurations of affliction and intellect. We experience the obscuration of affliction when the five afflictive emotions of ignorance, greed, aversion, pride, and jealousy are present in us; this prevents us from getting in touch with our true nature of selflessness. When we develop the four essential qualities of our heart and mind, we overcome the great delusion of affliction. We experience the obscuration of intellect when we become attached to different kinds of views and judgments; this prevents us from realizing omniscience. When we have transformed both kinds of obscuration, we attain omniscience.

How do we bring compassion love, joy, and equanimity into our actions? How do we cultivate them in the heart of our life, our body, speech, and mind? A wholesome attitude is the basic and most simple skillful means to stabilize our mind and perspective so we can reconnect with these qualities. When we stabilize our mind, it brings our body and speech into a state of harmony. Yet our body and mind have their own potential to change our attitude. Having a wholesome attitude is not enough, because sometimes there is a tendency of the mind to take us to an extreme. When anything falls into an extreme, it changes its nature. For example, we often try to prove that we are something we are not. This is the saddest thing we do to ourselves. We do this because our mind is asking it of us. We may be shy, but we try to be outgoing. We are getting old, but we try to be young. We like someone, but act as if we don't like him or her. We are in love, but resist it. In this constant process of pretense, we develop the conditioning of self-judgment. In the long run, we become addicted to self-judgment, which creates fear in our life.

We may shift from a wholesome attitude to an expectation without noticing. We may have a good motivation, but begin to grasp onto it and act out of that grasping. The moment we set up our motivation we have a tendency to become attached to a particular result. Our intention to be compassionate is there together with attachment. When we cling to a result, the energy is directed more strongly toward our expectation than toward the motivation itself. This begins to act as an obstacle for the motivation to manifest into action. This is where we need equanimity. When we have equanimity, we exhaust the conditioning that makes us cling to preferences. Then our motivation for love, compassion, and joy is not contaminated by expectations and attachment.

I have friends who are vegetarians. They don't like the idea of eating meat because one has to kill animals to get meat. I like that wholesome thought and the practice of not killing animals. However, vegetarianism can come from very different sources. It may be our compassion and our ability to see ourselves as not separate from all other beings that makes us feel we could not eat meat. Then, our compassion and our recognition of what compassion means can lead us to the nature of our mind. On the other hand, the idea of not eating meat may be attached to egotistic pride or fear. In that case, our attachment does not allow us to give space to compassion, love, and equanimity. Instead, we blame others and develop a feeling of hatred. In this process of judging and hating others we put ourselves into a state of misery. That is suffering. Any idea, concept, or attitude we hold onto without compassion, love, equanimity, and skillful knowledge is our ego of delusion. This ego destroys the essence of our wholesome attitude.

How do we feel when we see someone eating meat or buying meat at the market? What are the states of our mind, body, and emotions? Some of us distance ourselves from that situation or person; we might get angry with the person or become depressed. Sometimes we are hard on ourselves because of our subtle attachment to pride or ego without awareness. We may think we are better or that we are religious, environmentalist, vegetarian, or peace activists. We project our expectations onto others, thinking they should be acting according to what we think. What will happen if they don't? If we do not react under the influence of afflictions and feel compassion toward the other, then our response is an act of awakening. But if the other's action hurts our feelings, makes us depressed, or ties us up with chaotic emotions, this is not a wholesome practice. In this case we are inviting suffering into our life through our attachment to our ideas.

The same thing can occur with our attitude toward spiritual practice. Usually our mind is preoccupied with the experiences of daily life and we identify with them. We go on retreat to make it possible for our mind to be clear and free for the practice. But the kind of identification we usually have with the experiences of our daily lives can also be directed toward the practice. Our personal idea of practice can take us to an extreme that creates a resistance to anything other than the idea and concept of practice that we perceive. This is because we tend to become attached to our experiences. For this reason, when we have an experience of a blissful state, non-separateness, or the natural state of the mind, it is important that we do not hold on to it or judge ourselves for not being in that state any more. We tend to hold on to that state and want to remain in it. Because we are unable to do so, we condemn ourselves and experience disappointment, frustration, or even hatred toward ourselves. In this way, our experience of having had a glimpse of a profound and very beautiful state of mind can lead to the creation of more suffering.

This does not mean we should forget a deep experience we may have had. But we may create suffering for ourselves if we hold on to our experience in such a way that an expectation based on desire-attachment arises. We should try to recognize the value of such glimpses for our life and practice without letting this give rise to a wish to be somewhere other than where we are at this very moment. If we are unable to do this, we may have created duality out of a non-dual state. What we should do instead is use that particular experience to support our motivation for awakening so we do not judge our own experience or make it into a means for the creation of suffering. We bring all our experiences into the path of practice by appreciating them with neither attachment nor resistance. Then we can cultivate the mind and heart that allows us to simply be.

When we hold onto our motivation and expectations, we fall into extremes. For instance, we may fall into the extreme of thinking we are not good enough and become unwilling to receive anything from others. If we give, we have to receive too. We need to be forgiving and accepting with ourselves and with others. Self-compassion can help us avoid falling into the extreme of excluding ourselves from our compassion. The practice of receiving is self-compassion. Receiving does not mean we have to take something. It means we are able to live with the situation around us and make space in our hearts and minds for it. Sometimes our pride acts as a wall and does not allow us to experience the great gift of receiving. In particular, when we are in a difficult situation, we need to have compassion toward ourselves and remain strong so that our innate potential for healing can reveal itself.

Some years ago I was in a retreat where we did mountain walking. One day I was walking with a 72-year-old friend of mine along a winding creek. It was very beautiful, but to stay on the trail we had to cross the creek quite often. Once when we were crossing the creek, I asked my friend if she needed help. She stayed quiet and turned her face away from me. Unfortunately, she slipped and fell. We were both quiet and did not say anything, since it was a silent walking retreat. Later she fell down a second time. I was worried about her and so I extended my hand to help her get up. But she did not take my hand and said, "Tempa, as I was growing up I used to learn Aikido. So I know how to fall." I was happy to hear that because after her first fall I was preoccupied by my judgment about her age. At the same time I wanted to be helpful. When she fell down for the third time, I simply grabbed her and pulled her up. She looked at me and said, "Thank you, Tempa."

After our hike, during the meditation session at the temple I looked deeply into the nature of the incident. What stayed alive with me was the art of receiving. This gift can destroy the wall of pride and the fear that makes us weak.

THE INTERDEPENDENT NATURE OF ALL BEINGS

In order to actualize the way of a compassionate being and to cultivate the Intimate Mind we have to realize the great gift of inter-being, the interdependent nature of everything. Every sentient being comes to this earth through the womb and care of a great mother of love and compassion. Beyond the mother who gave birth to us, we can see many other elements of our life as our mother. The sun, the five elements, and the food that we eat, all give rise to our life and we depend on them, too. Recognizing this truth is very important for every step of the practice of a compassionate being. It can help us to see that at some point all beings have been our great mother of love and compassion. Then we can recognize all beings as a loving parent. Each being has been patient and compassionate with us and has given us this precious life. In remembering the kindness of each being toward us we develop a wish to serve and help all beings without excluding anyone. If we have the strong wish to help others, even if we are unable to do so, we will at least not harm others and ourselves, and we will not produce and foster a mind of ill intention toward others or the mind of weakness in ourselves. Our wish to help others has the power to free us from our afflictive habits that lead to harming others intentionally or unintentionally.

For some of us this simple method of practice might not

mean anything. Some of us may have no idea what a compassionate mother really means. We may have been a victim of misfortune and experienced a difficult childhood, difficult parents, a difficult marriage, or difficult children. For some of us, rather than nurturing our natural capacity to love and be open, our relationships may be a threat instead. Some of us may never have received loving care and compassion from anyone and never had an experience of compassion and love. In this case, the practice of generating the compassionate heart through the recognition of all beings as the loving mother of compassion might not appear possible. For the Intimate Mind, however, anything is possible.

We all want to be free from suffering and to be happy. In order to be happy, we have to recognize the causes of our distress. When we have recognized the causes, we work to let them go. Unless we let go of them we won't experience the true nature of eternal joy. It is often a difficult practice to let go of a situation that has brought us immense pain and suffering. Yet, we make our suffering even stronger by constantly visiting our memories and letting the pain and suffering we create control our life. Holding onto a situation, experience, or memory won't help us in freeing ourselves from suffering. Rather, it can become stronger and produce afflictive emotions such as hatred, anger, and depression in us. In this condition we lose our strength of confidence and become the victim of pain and suffering. By living with the disturbing nature of our past we destroy the miracle of each moment. This places us into a disturbed state of mind, and thus suffering continues.

It is important to realize that we are no longer living in the past but in the present moment. This is one way of cultivating a thought that will eventually turn us toward the development of skillful means we can use to free ourselves from the exhausting past experiences that constantly interrupt our peace of mind.

When we have had bad experiences with someone, it becomes difficult for us to connect with him or her again. However, the practice of a compassionate being is not about connecting with that person or that situation, but about connecting with ourselves, with our true state of love and compassion. When we can connect with ourselves with love and compassion, we will be able to see and feel our state of being with clarity. Often under the influence of past disturbances we cannot truly feel and acknowledge our potential gift within. Then, healing does not happen. Connecting with ourselves means recognizing the seeds of our suffering and working toward transformation.

How do we initiate this practice? Forgiveness and acceptance rooted in compassion and love are key for developing a new connection with others and with ourselves. We can open ourselves to forgiveness by contemplating the imperfect nature of all beings. We are all imperfect. We make mistakes under certain circumstances due to our lack of knowledge and understanding. The demanding nature of life and misfortune may force us to act in ways that are not in harmony with our wishes. We can contemplate that those who were not good to us might have been going through a bad time and this has caused them to act in an abusive manner toward us. They are also suffering and have become the victim of misfortune. With this thought we generate compassion for all beings who were, and maybe still are, lacking in skill and in the wisdom of compassion. If we can do this, it is one of the best gifts we can give to ourselves. This practice will reduce the emotional stress and suffering we may experience due to others' actions. It will deepen our own understanding of how painful it can be when we hurt someone's feelings or try to destroy their way of life. This realization is the essence of the practice of a compassionate being.

LOVE AND OPENNESS

When we have unconditional love, we wish that all beings may attain happiness. Because of our conditioning, the love we feel tends to include only the specific people who are close to us, specific objects, and specific preferences. That is conditional love. The conditions are the relationships we have with others. If we become aware of this and recognize the restrictions we impose on our love due to our conditioning, we can develop a quality of mind that has the natural capacity of equanimity, of seeing all beings with the same eyes. Then our very feeling of love for someone does not become a seed for desire-attachment that is directed toward a particular person, being, or phenomenon. Rather, it becomes genuinely inclusive. In order to do this we have to be stable and strongly motivated. We have to be stable so that fear does not carry us away, and we have to be strongly motivated so that we can love ourselves and drop our fear and self-judgment. If we judge ourselves, we are not open and cannot really love others.

We tend to suppress our confidence. We think we are not good enough, or that we should not attempt something because we believe we cannot do it well enough or do not have enough knowledge. If we feel this way, we need the motivation and strength to be honest and real with respect to our situation and to external conditions. This will enable us to bring ourselves out of the constriction of self-judgment. Then we can see that we are not separate from others and drop our fear, self-judgment, and the projected judgment of others. This will allow us to feel compassion and love for ourselves.

Usually we live within this constriction of self-judgment because our perception of others and ourselves involves comparison. For instance, when we meet a wonderful practitioner and see his or her qualities of heart and mind, this can touch and move us deeply. But our appreciation of this person's qualities of heart and mind can also become a causal seed for self-judgment. When this happens, we begin to feel guilty; we feel we are not good enough and lose contact with the Intimate Mind. This may develop an exhausting feeling of jealousy that takes us further away from our own inherent quality of equanimity and our compassionate heart. This is why we need strength, mental stability, and a wholesome motivation. These qualities enable us to feel, experience, and see the realm outside of our judgment. Having freed ourselves from judgment, we can move forward in the direction that will eliminate the dividing line that separates the two realms. We will be able to see with equanimity and openness.

The capacity for our heart to be open is essential to our ability to love and to feel compassion. Openness is the act of providing space for others and ourselves to be who we really are. When we are open, we live with the experience of each moment. Sometimes our conditioning and fear do not allow our openness to fully manifest. We close our heart because of ignorance. Yet, suffering is more likely when our heart is not open. With a closed heart we cannot reach the essence and the gifts of other beings and be of mutual benefit to each other. When we are closed, we cannot recognize and feel the openness of others. This turns the other into an object of fear and that causes us suffering. When we are not open, we experience doubt. In the presence of doubt we begin to judge everything. This leads to mistrust, wrong views, separation, and fear, which isolate us from others and from life. Living with this isolation can be suffocating.

Openness can also produce fear and suffering. If we are open but not emotionally stable, there is a tendency to get distracted by external objects or by the behavior of others. If we are open but emotionally insecure, our openness can take us to a vulnerable place. We can be easily hurt by our own openness because we tend to get absorbed by the overwhelming suffering of situations that we encounter. Our witnessing of the pain and suffering of others stirs up our own emotional conditioning. We may carry this with us for a long time. Unable to recognize what is happening in us, we enter into a state of depression instead of giving rise to compassion and being able to make a positive difference.

Another obstacle to openness arises from having too many expectations. If our openness is carried away by our expectations, there is grasping or subtle desire-attachment. If our openness is due to expectations, these expectations will become a hindrance and prevent our openness from manifesting its true nature. Our attachment to our expectations will cause suffering rather than help us actualize the true nature of openness.

When our openness is mixed with expectations or with emotional instability, it is no longer true openness. These corrupted forms of openness are not helpful for others or ourselves in the process of the transformation of suffering. In the teachings of Yungdrung Bön, the word *Yungdrung* is a union of the two words *yung* and *drung*. *Yung* means the absolute unborn truth, and *drung* denotes the unaffected, self-arising nature of phenomena. The unification of these two qualities is the true nature of all phenomena. As for our own mind and body, when we are less affected by distraction, there is less diversion from the true nature of our mind. Our practice is to develop a quality of strength that supports us to stay unaffected. Staying unaffected can be misleading here. The Intimate Mind is beyond the duality of affected and unaffected. We do our best not to be affected by negativity and by anything that is obscured by delusion. At the same time we have the ability to stay open to the nurturing qualities that we need to awaken. When we surpass the conditioning of duality, we embody the spirit of Yungdrung Bön. If we can cultivate a quality of openness based on stability, strength, and clarity, we are in a position to move beyond being affected by the pain and suffering of ourselves and others. The stability and strength of our openness will allow us to move on, and it will direct us toward the transformation of the suffering we see.

CULTIVATING COMPASSION

Clearing the conditioning
that separates us
from the rest of the world
is true compassion.
It is the wish
that all beings may be free from suffering.

The openness and compassion that are at the heart of the aspiration of the Intimate Mind include all beings—not just one or two beings, and not just the people who are close to us. With the Intimate Mind we turn toward all beings, including those we perceive as our enemies. Can we have a heart and mind that reflect the all-pervasive nature of the vast blue sky, a heart and mind that are able to reach and include every sentient being on this earth, in particular those who are obscured by afflictions and imprisoned by the resulting suffering?

From the perspective of the Intimate Mind, every sentient being is included in our path of practice. Otherwise, we will obscure the aspiration of attaining our true awakened nature. If we feel compassion for someone and want to benefit him or her, but at the same time we don't want to benefit someone else, there is a distinction and therefore duality. When there is duality, it narrows the space available for our openness, compassion, and unconditional love. We may wish to help our relatives, family, and friends. Our love and care for them keeps our relationship with them healthy and strong, and it can give us a lot of strength. But our life is not just about our relatives. We encounter many people besides our family and our loved ones. Due to the interdependent nature of all beings, if our compassion and loving care only extend to certain people and not to others, we are sowing a seed and creating conditioning that ultimately leads us to suffering rather than to the realization of our true nature.

When we aspire to embrace all beings in our compassion, we open the door of the miracle of each moment regardless of whether we are experiencing distress or joy. A simple, powerful practice for generating the aspiration of a compassionate being is to bring everything into the field of our awareness. We do not limit this to living beings, but include also the elements of earth, water, fire, air, and space that have been nurturing our life force. The masculine lunar energy and feminine solar energy have made evolution possible. Remembering these great energy sources and their gifts of love, care, compassion, and vital life force energy helps us to gain understanding into the interdependent nature of all phenomena and to make our aspiration more all-encompassing.

Remembering the gifts of other beings and of the great sources of life to us, we can ask in what way we could make better use of the gifts we have received. We can ask what gift we could offer in return for their immense kindness. This can inspire us to give rise to the aspiration to refrain from anything that is initiated or carried out under the obscuration of ignorance, greed, envy, desire-attachment, anger, or fear.

Another practice for generating the mind and heart of a compassionate being is to bring someone who is going through a difficult time, a situation of destruction, war, or killing into our mind and heart. We look deeply into the nature of their pain and suffering and generate the deep feeling of non-separateness, so that our heart and mind can open. Letting your heart and mind break open through touching the pain and suffering of another is an aspect of compassion. However, if we let the pain we witness affect us, we will become the victim of the situation and a victim of our own fear. We need wisdom to know if we are ready to take on another's pain. Compassion needs to be accompanied by strength and wisdom so that we are able to bear the suffering we witness and to have the understanding needed to help others.

Sometimes, a feeling of compassion can imply duality. For instance, we have compassion for the squirrel that is being chased by the dog. Based on our conditioning, our feelings of love and care for the squirrel make us feel hatred for the dog on a subconscious level. That is ignorance. We have to be able to witness what the hatred we feel for the dog does to our heart and mind. This is why, when we bring a situation of suffering into our mind and heart, it is important that we bring our awareness to the suffering of all those involved without distinction, and to the ignorance that is causing their actions. Seeing the ignorance that is affecting all beings and causing pain to themselves and others, our wish is that they may be free from ignorance.

As we open our heart to all beings, the natural unconditional love and compassion of our innate nature can emerge from the treasure box hidden within us. In the beginning we do this exercise with someone we feel close to, someone we love or feel connected to. Later when we feel more comfortable and more at ease with this practice, we extend it to all beings throughout space and time. This can be a powerful practice that we should not underestimate. Even if we do it for just two minutes every day, the miracle of continuous practice imprints the qualities of this practice of compassion into our hearts and minds. A bird flying in and out of a cave has left a mark of its wing on the stone. Even a small drop of water, if dripping continuously, can make a hole in a rock. We, too, can make out of our practice whatever we want, if our motivation, the seed for this path, is strong.

It is important that our motivation is born from the wish to help all beings, including ourselves. Sometimes in search of others' well-being we forget ourselves. We become hard on ourselves, and we become overly sensitive. We put ourselves into a vulnerable state of both mind and emotion. We need to first make ourselves strong and stable mentally, emotionally, and physically. In order to do so, we have to accept our suffering, no matter what we are going through at that moment, with great compassion and self-care. Otherwise, the overwhelming intensity of suffering in the world might burn us. If one does not know how to swim, but jumps into the river, one will be carried away with the river's flow.

CHAPTER 3

ASPIRING TO THE INTIMATE MIND

RECOGNIZING OUR INNATE POTENTIAL

Every sentient being has an innate potential to awaken, in the same way that every seed has the potential to replicate its essence in the forms of fruit or tree. But this potential is hidden by a dense cloud of ignorance and the conditioning of emotions such as anger, self-centeredness, fear, and self-judgment—what we call afflictive emotions. Too often, we give power to these emotions and allow them to keep us from what is possible. We have to go beyond these afflictive emotions to manifest our nature and bring our true potential for goodness into every situation we engage in.

When we recognize our innate potential, we also respect all beings (including ourselves) and we respect their unique qualities. If we do this, we can bring our innate potential for goodness into our speaking, thinking, and actions. In order for anything to manifest its true nature, a deeper sense of interdependence needs to be brought into play. This is genuine and possible. You and I and many others are needed for the manifestation of this moment—this is what I mean by "inter-being." The elements that make our present moment possible include not just ourselves, but also many other beings and conditions.

Let me offer an example. An olive has the potential to give olive oil, but just knowing about this potential is not enough; it does not bring forth the result directly. However, recognizing this potential as its nature allows us to apply a skillful means so that the olive can manifest its quality in the form of oil. This allows us to bring forth the qualities of the olive in a manifested form. The first step in this process is the recognition that the olive has the potential to give olive oil. When we have recognized that the olive has this potential, we open our minds toward the possibility of applying a particular skillful means that corresponds to the potential nature of olive oil and its manifestation in an active form. We may have to press the olive, chop it, mash it, or process it in a machine to get the oil, but the first thing we must do is recognize that the olive has that potential. If we press a stone we will not get olive oil, no matter how hard we press. This is because the stone does not have the innate potential of olive oil. No matter how hard we press it, it is not going to manifest what we are looking for.

When I say that we all have the potential to awaken, what is it that we are awakening from? Sometimes we experience pain, and sometimes joy and happiness. Some of us experience suffering almost continuously. The Bön Buddhist belief is that suffering and happiness exist within the nature of all beings. But life is not made up only of suffering and happiness. It also has its essence, which is our potential to recognize our pain and happiness and to make a choice about what to renounce and what to cultivate. Having the potential to awaken means that we can recognize what causes our suffering and the suffering we see in others' lives. We tend to think our suffering comes from outside ourselves and that someone else has to solve our problems or help us. But actually it is we ourselves who have this capacity. Since we have the potential to awaken, we can free ourselves from our suffering.

When we recognize our potential to awaken, this recognition can give us the strength to wake up for our own benefit and for that of others. Sometimes we are so discouraged by the continuous flow of circumstances and by the demanding nature of suffering and of life itself that we lose our strength. We learn to live with the suffering because we do not recognize the causes of our situation and consequently cannot recognize our potential for change. We have become so used to our suffering that we unconsciously assume it will always remain with us. Yet, each and every thing has its causes. These causes can change, just like everything else in our lives. When a cause ends, so will its effects. To transform our suffering, we have to know what is causing it. When we recognize and accept the causes, the path to transforming our suffering is revealed. Our innate potential to awaken recognizes the suffering and its causes and gives us confidence that we are able to transform it.

We humans are among the most fortunate beings on this planet. We have the gift of our human form with a mind that can understand and recognize its own true nature and show us the unique qualities of our human nature. The mind and heart we are gifted with make it possible for us to connect with all beings and to value the gifts and blessings that each of them brings to this world. When we do this, we lay the foundation to help other beings connect with their own true nature. That is why our human life is so precious. We have the ability to understand the causes of suffering, and with the compassion of our hearts, the ability to reduce it.

THE HEART THAT EMBRACES SUFFERING

We are motivated to transform our suffering and to awaken when we recognize suffering in our own lives and in the lives of others and understand its causes. At the heart of this recognition are love and acceptance. The capacity to transform suffering, whether our own or that of others, lies in our loving and compassionate heart. We need this heart so that we can recognize suffering without feeling discouraged, giving rise to aversion, or letting the suffering take away our peace of mind. We let the suffering itself motivate us to work toward its transformation. If we don't recognize suffering, we cannot have compassion. Without compassion we will not be able to recognize the presence of suffering and achieve its transformation. The recognition of suffering, the arising of compassion, and the aspiration to help others and oneself find liberation are at the heart of the path that was taught and lived by the Bön Buddha Tonpa Shenrab* and the Buddhas of other times.

Knowing that all beings, including ourselves, suffer and feel pain, we need to accept and embrace that fact. This is the first step. Our acceptance of our own situation and of the suffering of others enables us to cultivate great compassion toward all beings. When we have seen, experienced, and realized the pain and suffering of this world, we need to find a space within ourselves

---

* Tonpa Shenrab is the enlightened teacher who taught the teachings of Yungdrung Bön. He is said to have lived approximately 18,000 years before our time.

where we can connect with our true nature and take refuge in it and in the awakened heart and mind of a compassionate being. We should not let the pain and suffering that we see and experience dominate our consciousness, but we should let it help us connect with our innate potential to be more accepting and more skillful. We may feel hopeless or overwhelmed by the pain and suffering that we see. When we are affected in this way, we lose the space within ourselves that generates compassion, forgiveness, and kindness, and we instead become one with the suffering. Instead, we should do our best to witness the pain and suffering that we see, let it touch our heart and mind, and let it connect us with our compassion and our understanding of the ignorance that affects all sentient beings. When we do this, we take refuge in our compassionate heart, and in the qualities that can forgive others and enable us to be of help to others and ourselves.

Taking refuge is essential to the path of compassionate beings. In the Bön Buddhist teachings we take refuge in the Buddha—or our own awakened potential and the awakened nature of all beings. We take refuge in the Dharma or truth, the eternal teachings on the path that lead us to awakening. And we take refuge in the companionship of all beings who walk the path with us. In order to take refuge in the awakened nature of all beings, we must develop trust in this awakened nature and in the qualities of awakening. This enables us to be more deeply and continuously aware of our own potential for awakening so that we can become a refuge for others. Taking refuge in the teachings on the path of compassionate beings helps us to cultivate trust in our own potential of wisdom and in the wisdom of the teachings. Taking refuge in the companionship of all beings also means we understand that we depend on each other. This helps us to be more accepting and forgiving if a situation works out differently than we expected.

In taking refuge, we commit to wholesome actions of our body, speech, and mind. Taking refuge in our awakened nature, we take refuge in our wholesome mind, a mind that is free of thoughts that harm others or ourselves. Taking refuge in the Dharma, we take refuge in speech that is kind and honest. Taking refuge in the companionship of all beings, we commit to not harming each other through our actions.

When we take refuge, the objects of our refuge become a source of our strength, wisdom, and compassion. Whenever we feel overwhelmed by suffering, or become distracted or angry, we can remember these sources of refuge and return to them. When we see suffering and pain, we recognize it and develop the wish to be free of it and to help others be free as well. We take refuge in this wish, and in our potential to be free.

When we take refuge, it is like coming home. Through taking refuge we lay the foundations for our path to cultivate an unconditional wish to help all beings according to our capacity. There are many different ways to work toward this realization and to help others as a compassionate being. Within Bön Buddhism, we say that there are 84,000 different ways to realize one's true nature and to help others. This is because we are all different and need different approaches.

On the path of a compassionate being, there will always be obstacles and difficulties. In order to be able to meet these, we must not expect too much of ourselves. It is also important that we do not project our expectations onto others about how they should be or how they should act. When we resist these tendencies, we can stay in touch with our open heart and with the mind of no fear. The mind of no fear is the awakened mind. This will give us the strength and confidence that we need to move on.

THE ASPIRATION OF A COMPASSIONATE BEING

Realizing the suffering
caused by unwholesome actions of body, speech, and mind
we develop the wish to renounce them.
Realizing the gift of wholesome practice,
we cultivate the wish to actualize it.
Seeing the suffering of all beings,
the wish arises
to free ourselves and others from suffering,
and to help all beings
attain liberation into our true nature.

The Intimate Mind aspires to fully awaken and to help others attain this realization. This aspiration arises in us through our deep love and compassion for others and for ourselves, and through reflection on the pain and suffering we encounter and experience every day of our lives. This aspiration is more than a mere wish to end suffering. We must bring our recognition of suffering and our compassionate heart together with our understanding of the nature of cause and effect. We need to look deeply into the nature of our suffering and into what obscures us from our awakened nature.

We have to understand the distinction between wholesome actions and unwholesome actions. Unwholesome actions always create suffering, whether for ourselves or for others, whether direct or indirect. The suffering we cause to ourselves through our actions can be twofold. It can be in the form of karmic consequences, or it can take the form of bringing up afflictive emotions and reinforcing a conditioning related to that emotion. For example, stealing is considered an unwholesome action in the Bön tradition. Stealing may not bring immediate suffering to the person who is stealing. However we do experience its karmic consequences in the form of ignorance, attachment, or addiction or by becoming a victim of guilt. In addition, before we steal or carry out some other unwholesome action, we may go through an inner struggle that causes us conscious or unconscious suffering. The process of preparing ourselves to be a means of unwholesome actions is itself suffering.

Unwholesome actions include not just actions of our body, but also actions of our speech and actions of our mind. For example, lying is an unwholesome action of our speech and having ill intention toward someone is an unwholesome action of our mind. While the suffering we create for ourselves through an unwholesome action of mind may seem more apparent and immediate, this effect is also present with unwholesome actions of speech and body.

When we recognize that wholesome actions bring happiness and unwholesome actions bring suffering, a shift can take place in our mind. On the basis of this recognition, we begin to see how obscuration arises due to our holding on to the material reality that is surrounding us, and our belief in an inherently existing, separate self-identity. When we know that this obscuration is shared by all beings, we can turn our mind away from clinging to this self-identity. We can begin to feel compassion for all sentient beings who are obscured in this way just like us. By recognizing this fact, we begin to follow the path of wholesome actions. This very thought is the aspiration of a compassionate being.

When we have formed this aspiration, we need to trust in it. Our trust is based on the stability of our mind and the openness and presence of our heart. When we trust our aspiration and our capacity, a genuine loving confidence can arise. This loving confidence is the wish to actualize our aspiration. When we have developed this wish, our path of practice is to gradually bring it into all of daily life and make it continuous through the presence and openness of our mind. To have presence of mind, we must observe our actions; to have openness, we must trust not only our own awakened nature, but the awakened and selfless nature of all beings. We recognize them as our spiritual friends and companions who are helping us walk this path and realize our true nature. It is not just those who are close to us and who give us love and support who help us, but also those to whom we may respond with afflictive reactions. If somebody makes us angry or jealous, he or she is helping us by pointing out who we are at that moment and helping us to see ourselves more clearly. It is when we are not open that we take these incidents as disturbing. But when our heart and mind are open, we realize how much these moments can help us see into the nature of cause and effect.

Our heart and mind have the innate potential to feel unconditional love and compassion for all beings. It is through these innate qualities that we bring our aspiration into all of our life. To connect with our innate love for all beings, we need to form the intention that whatever love we feel may be directed toward all beings. Then, our path of practice is to live by this aspiration and by our love for all beings. This directs our love toward the nature of the whole of reality. Our love begins to exist without reference toward any particular object, and we eventually realize the selfless nature of all beings.

Sometimes the aspiration we form can challenge us and make us question our capacity to actualize it. If we feel this way, can we hold this thought gently and lovingly without judging ourselves? Offering ourselves this acceptance gives us strength and space for unconditional love and compassion and for the aspiration of a compassionate being to arise within us. By holding this thought with loving acceptance we unify completely with our situation as it is. We stop struggling, wanting to be different and hiding our weaknesses from ourselves and others. At the same time, when we can completely accept ourselves as we are, we find we no longer feel a need to judge others. We can let go of our addiction to constantly keeping ourselves protected from any suffering and pain. This may be one of the greatest obstacles we face on the path of a compassionate being. Due to our delusions, self-centeredness, and self-judgment, most of us will not realize our innate potential without facing suffering. When we can find the openness and strength of our heart and mind to embrace our suffering, we have made space for the aspiration of a compassionate being to arise naturally in us.

This is not to say that it is necessary to suffer in order to realize our true nature. If we encounter compassionate beings and experience their love and the way they live their lives, this can point our mind toward our own true nature. Another's selfless love can awaken the same selfless love in us.

Opening our heart to the aspiration of a compassionate being is an ongoing process. At many moments, our heart opens more than before. Can we nourish gratitude in ourselves for this miracle? When our heart opens, it changes us. Feelings come and go, and even our understanding comes and leaves again as it is replaced by deeper understanding. Seeds are planted in us by those moments when we experience true compassion and recognize our non-separateness from all beings. With patience we will find that those seeds continuously give rise to compassion and a stronger ability to express love and compassion in our life. This is because unconditional compassion and love are our true nature.

THE MOTIVATION OF THE INTIMATE MIND

The aspiration of the Intimate Mind points the way for us. Yet without the motivation to make it manifest, our aspiration will remain just an idea. Motivation is the potential that can bring changes into our life. Motivation is the thought that turns the mind toward its essence. It is the basic inherent goodness of the human being, the unification of the mind of wisdom and the open heart. This unification allows us to recognize the true nature of our being.

Whenever we want to start something new, it must begin with a thought that motivates us and has the power to manifest into action. The thought which motivates and the thought that manifests the action can be twofold: The first is the causal motivation. The second is the motivation at the time of actual action, or the motivation of action.

What gives birth to causal motivation or wholesome thought? From the perspective of the nature of the mind, motivation is just a simple thought; it is neither wholesome, nor unwholesome. This thought can arise from compassion and goodwill, or it could be governed by the chaotic, dispersed energy of our conditioning. This is what makes the thought different in terms of its nature and its resulting impact. For instance, you may have seen a homeless person on the street and at that very moment your primary consciousness is turned toward that homeless person. This is because the other's situation has touched you and has broken open your heart. At that very moment, your heart is breaking because the situation you encounter is allowing you to touch your true nature.

The causal motivation of a compassionate being arises from our true nature. Due to distraction and lack of stability and wholesome motivation, we become disconnected from that nature. If we let the experiences of our life touch us in this way, whether they are wholesome or painful and filled with suffering, they will create a space within us. And once we have developed the aspiration to transform the suffering we witness, the causal motivation of a compassionate being can manifest through this space. What is this causal motivation? It is selflessness. While external objects and incidences can help this causal motivation to manifest, the intention we bring to the situation plays the larger role. The external situation functions as a reminder, as a mirror that reflects our own face to us.

Sometimes we get stuck in our wish to help others. Without realizing it, we may be carrying out our practice simply because it makes us feel good and comfortable. We may develop a feeling of comfort and resonance with the state of mind we connect with through our practice and begin to feel a need for this state of mind. Then our motivation to do our practice is actually based on our wish toward self-fulfillment. Instead of clearing the causal seeds of our afflictions, we are again nurturing our conditioning.

How can we ensure that our initial motivation to become a compassionate being has the capacity to manifest into action without becoming dominated by our wish for self-fulfillment? This is an important question to ask when we want to engage in the path of a compassion being and transform ourselves. Our motivation can have the power to manifest into action, transforming the conditioning of our habitual patterns and the behavior that has brought us immense pain and suffering, but this is not easy. In our practice there is both our motivation and a shadow that is constantly trying to exhaust us. Our afflictive conditioning may be so strong that it takes over our motivation to become a compassionate being. Then, our motivation does not serve anymore as a pure and wholesome force, but instead feeds our afflictive conditioning and causes us suffering.

This shadow in our motivation is often not really affected by the calmness of mind we can find through meditation. We must be clear about whether it is this calmness we are seeking or whether we want to truly transform ourselves. Again and again, we need to look more closely at what our motivation to practice is. We have to be clear about why we are practicing. Why are we meditating? Why do we want to help others? Why do we want to be activists? Why do we aspire to be compassionate beings?

If we do not know what our motivation is, we may unwillingly sow a seed that gives rise to suffering. Our practice may exhaust us or not really change us even after many years of practice. We need to examine our motivation with the strength of heart and mind to accept that our shadow is present alongside it. Through our honesty and acceptance we can become familiar with ourselves, with the arising of our emotions, with the way we live and with what is it to be sitting in the face of depression. When we become this familiar with ourselves, we develop a heart to accept and embrace what we find inside us.

I would like to tell you a story about a moment in my life that taught me about motivation. This happened when I was maybe 12 or 13 years old living in Menri monastery in Dolanji as a monk. Every morning for breakfast each monk would get one piece of Tibetan bread. The first morning when I was in charge of the younger monks as a monitor, someone came to give me a piece of bread. When I looked at the bread, I saw that it wasn't cooked well. It was sticky and wet. I knew this uncooked bread would sit in my stomach all morning until lunch, so I decided I would not eat it. I rolled the bread into a ball, looked around and then threw it away.

Fortunately our abbot saw this. He walked toward me and said, "Tempa, what did you do? I saw you were throwing something away."

Wanting to be honest with him I answered, "The bread wasn't cooked right, so I didn't feel like eating it and I threw it away."

Our abbot responded, "Well, you don't have to do that. You can ask that it be baked again. Do you know that?"

When he said that, it touched my heart and produced a strong feeling of gratitude in me for the love and generosity of many beings that had made it possible for this food to manifest. It reminded me of the many times when he talked about his friends in the West who support Menri monastery. He would talk about their generosity and their contribution to the running of Menri. "You have no idea how the food comes to you. You throw it away simply because it isn't cooked."

That was a very special moment in my life. It changed my way of thinking forever. This incident gave birth to a very simple thought in me that turned my whole being toward the well-being of others. These others do not have to be living beings. They can be anything, including a piece of bread. It is such a beautiful practice to cultivate the heart and mind that acknowledges the importance of others' presence in our lives and the difference that their presence makes. This understanding is the turning point of the Bön Buddhist teachings of awakening. If we acknowledge the value of all the different elements in our life, this reduces the causal conditions that give rise to ill intentions, and instead nourishes our capacity to love and respect and to meet the world with an open heart.

PART II

SUFFERING AND TRANSFORMATION

CHAPTER 4

DISTRACTION

Many of us engage in a spiritual path and practice in order to find a way to experience less suffering in our life and to be happier. We need to look deeply into our longing for spiritual practice so that we know and understand what we want and what we are looking for. If we want our spiritual practice to make positive changes in our life, we have to understand the elements in us that give rise to our suffering and our happiness. We have to be aware of the causes of suffering in us.

When we feel our practice is not working toward the transformation of our suffering, we may judge the practice for not being effective, or we may blame the circumstances of our life. Sometimes we expect too much from our practice. Expectation creates a separation between us and the essence of the practice. It turns our practice into distraction. When the practice becomes a distraction, it cannot transform us. We have to stay connected with the practice in such a way that we also remain connected with the state of our being and the feelings we are dealing with. We need to integrate the practice with the state of our being. If we do not truly accept the state of our being as it is, the causes of our suffering remain in place, and transformation is not possible.

What is it that we have to accept? We have to accept the state of our mind and emotions at each moment. We accept ourselves with a sense of self-care and gentleness. Acceptance directs our awareness toward the state of our being. Once our awareness becomes one with the state of our being, we recognize our situation. Knowing and awareness are different. We may know that something is causing us suffering, but we may not be aware of this in every moment. This is due to our distraction in the form of judgment, rejection, attachment, or fear. Our distraction prevents us from actualizing what we know. For example, we may know that smoking is not good for our health. However, while we are smoking, we are not aware of the negative consequences of smoking. This is because distraction in the form of our habit of addiction comes between our awareness and our actions.

True acceptance is without judgment, rejection, or fear. This is why we have to know clearly what is motivating us to practice and what we are really looking for. We may be practicing to enhance our knowledge. If this is our motivation, our practice will help us gain knowledge, but it may not help us take care of our afflictive emotions. Or we may be practicing because of a problem that is causing us suffering. In this case, the practice may help us address our problem, but we may lack the motivation to transform our life. We have to be honest with ourselves about why we are practicing.

If we practice with the motivation to truly transform our suffering, our afflictive emotions and habits, and to become a compassionate being, our practice will help us to do this. If we know that this is why we are practicing, this will give us the strength to look into the state of our being, our suffering and its causes, and to accept what is causing us suffering with gentleness and compassion. Without true acceptance, our denial won't allow us to see what causes our suffering. As long as we deny our suffering, its causes will remain hidden to us. It is these causes that are at the root of our suffering. If we do not go to the root of our suffering, anything we do to try to get rid of it is at best a temporary fix. Without recognizing the causes of our suffering, transformation cannot take place. When we reach a place where we are able to experience deep acceptance of our situation and the causes of our state of being, the door toward numerous possibilities of transformation opens. Through our acceptance and awareness we can recognize whether the state of our being is causing us happiness or pain and suffering. If it is feeding our conditioning and giving us suffering, then we can use our practice to let it go. The first step is to recognize our own situation and our problems. From there we can turn toward spiritual practice.

THE STATE OF DISTRACTION

There are many different kinds of distraction. We may get distracted when we see or hear something, or when we think of something. Sometimes, the wandering of our mind takes us far away from its true nature. The further we move, the more we disconnect from its qualities. In this process we may lose our connection to the Intimate Mind. From the Bön Buddhist view, distraction means disconnecting from our true nature. A sound we hear or an object we see is not a distraction from our true nature. The distraction is our reaction to an object on the basis of our conditioning, because of our anger, our jealousy, our insecurity, or our desire-attachment. Or it may be a sense of separateness, such as when we think we are different from others because of our race, our religion, or our economic situation. Feeling different from others creates a sense of separateness. We are also distracted when we speak in a way that hurts others, through telling lies, using harsh speech, or cursing. Why is cursing distraction? I see cursing as a distraction because it takes our mind away from our true nature. We curse because we are distracted. From the viewpoint of the Intimate Mind, we do not speak in a way that hurts someone because we are not separate from one another.

It is important to observe the nature of the distraction we experience in each moment. We need to observe how often we get distracted in the same manner. Does it happen only once every few years, once a month, once a week, or every ten seconds? Through observing our distraction we become familiar with its nature and its causes. We react because of our conditioning. Our reaction creates a separation from the nature of our mind. This separation causes suffering.

Distraction also impairs the cognitive capacity of our mind by causing obstacles and obscurations to the true nature of our mind that prevent it from perceiving and experiencing directly without distortion. Distraction is the displacement of the object of our attention. Distraction is anything that comes between the mind and the object of the mind, breaking our concentration on the object and preventing us from becoming one with it.

If the mind is completely unobscured, it is in its natural state. It will then perceive everything exactly as it is without any reaction that disturbs the natural state. Once we have recognized this, we can train our mind to increase our capacity to be in its natural state and to reduce the power distraction has over us. We do this by training ourselves to be more aware of every situation we encounter and of the way we respond to it. In doing this, we gradually increase the power of our awareness. Through this awareness we come to know ourselves intimately. This brings us in touch with the Intimate Mind.

HABITUAL DISTRACTION

We can practice awareness throughout our daily lives. Usually, we keep ourselves busy with our work, family and friends, the TV, our computer and email, video games, and other sources of entertainment. We think that these things keep our life in order. Many of us operate from this perspective. We continually feel as though we need something to keep our mind occupied, and when there is nothing immediately available, we feel affected, we feel restless, frustrated, lonely, or guilty for not doing anything. We are not usually aware that feelings of guilt are distracting us from our true nature and creating the need for further distraction. The feeling of guilt is a distraction to the Intimate Mind because it is a subtle form of suffering.

We are also not aware of how our need for distraction affects the way we live. In fact, we prepare our mind and body to feel this kind of need. Without noticing, we create a habit of constant distraction. Our attachment to outer form and inner emotions develops a habit of constant need to be attached to something, involved with something, listening to, looking at, or thinking about something. When our mind becomes obsessed with something, this obsession acts as a repetitive source of distraction.

Distraction in the form of habitual craving may not be very active or strong all the time. However, it remains present in our consciousness. Since it is in our stream of consciousness, we experience it when we encounter corresponding external sense objects, internal memories, or physical needs. These encounters activate our habit and make it stronger. As our habit becomes more dominating, our body, mind, and feelings support it and lose their own essence. This is the greatest distraction to the nature of our mind. For example, there may be someone we dislike. If we do not recognize our feelings of dislike and their effect on our mind, we may gradually feel that our dislike or hatred is justified. At this point, our dislike is supported directly by our mind and a habit is formed.

When our mind, feelings, and body support our habit, this prevents us from recognizing the nature and effect of our habit. Then, we cannot trust our own inner wisdom about what is good for us and make a distinction whether a situation is based on our conditioning of desire-attachment or our good will. We may have a feeling, for instance, that a situation is not good for us, but we are not able to trust this feeling because our habitual conditioning is so strong that it impairs our mind and distracts our feelings. Then, our feelings begin to support our habitual conditioning and make it stronger. The effect on our mind is that it is carried away by our addictive habit and becomes so unstable that it constantly moves from one object to another in the search of joy, love, calmness, and peace.

Addiction is the belief that we need something to such an extent that our happiness depends on it. In addition to the kinds of addiction we usually think of in this context, this could also include our addiction to work, to our mental fantasies, to the notion of having popcorn and watching movies, or to things happening in a certain way. Under the influence of addictive habits, we begin to struggle with confusion and despair because we do not know the cause of our afflictive feelings and how to free ourselves from them. The more confused and desperate we feel, the more this narrows our strength of taking initiative toward transformation. We feel tightness around our heart, and our mind gets trapped in that tightness. We are no longer able to see the true state of our being. Under the possession of our conditioning, we disconnect from ourselves and from the world around us. Even if we know the state of our being, we might not be able to accept it because we feel powerless and frightened. We become a victim of mental and emotional chaos and afflictive emotions. We blame either ourselves and our perceived lack of strength, or the demanding nature of the circumstances of our life for how we are feeling. In this way, we disconnect from our inherent self-confidence, which is the very potential we need to heal our life.

The insecurity and instability of our mind and feelings caused by habitual conditioning can force us to engage in unwholesome actions in order to meet our habitual needs. These harmful actions bring suffering and pain into our life and the lives of others. We may think the way we are responding is okay or right, and we never see it from the other side. We never see that our emotional reaction will not be able to affect the situation positively, and we never see what another's feelings might be or whether our action might go against their feelings.

Sometimes we do not want to know the causes of our habitual conditioning. This very habit is itself a distraction for our mind and heart from their awakened nature. In order to protect ourselves from judgment, we may give numberless reasons for our behavior. We do this because we know we have become the victim of insecurity and self-judgment, weakness, shame, or guilt. This makes it even more difficult to face the inner battle of self-hatred and the external battle of protection from the judgment of others. We may feel that no one will be able to help us. However, we are the ones who have the ability to help ourselves with the quality of awareness that is unified with self-care and self-compassion. The qualities of self-care and self-compassion have the strength that will take us beyond the grasp of habitual conditioning.

When there is suffering and pain, there is a cause for it. If there is a cause, there is also a way that leads out of suffering. This way exists before we even encounter suffering. Sometimes the suffering and the situation that give rise to it are so intense and overwhelming that they take over our mind. When we are under the influence of an overwhelming experience of pain and suffering, it is all we can see, feel, and think. We do not see its causes and the way of cessation and, in fact, may not accept its existence even if someone explains it to us.

The way of the Intimate Mind is not to blame ourselves or our circumstances. Rather, we try to find the heart and mind to recognize our weakness without judgment. We accept our weakness and look thoroughly into its nature so that we can understand its causes and how it affects us. This understanding forms the basis for transformation. If we only recognize our weakness without recognizing its causes and consequences in our life, this will not have much effect. It is through awareness based on compassion and self-care that we become able to recognize the causes and consequences of our suffering and the way of transformation.

It is very important to not become the victim of external judgment and self-hatred, but rather to look deeply into the nature of our behavior and our state of being. We have to be honest and authentic with ourselves, with our problem, and with our self-judgment. This is the beginning of developing the strength of genuine self-acceptance. This acceptance is not just about accepting ourselves as the victim of a strong habit or conditioning. Rather, it means that we open our heart and mind to accept the damage, pain, and suffering caused by our habitual conditioning. By doing this we can bring the missing link between our true nature and our corrupted state of mind back into our life.

Self-acceptance of this nature is much harder to develop than to just accept that we have a problem. Once we have the strength to completely accept our habitual conditioning and to be fully aware of its consequences, we can become familiar with it. We will no longer feel overwhelmed by it and can begin to generate a sense of self-caring. This quality of self-care naturally leads to the development of self-compassion. Self-compassion allows us to give a space to ourselves and our conditioning, and to see the part of ourselves that is being damaged by our conditioning and the behavior that it causes.

In the beginning it is very important just to notice our conditioning. Once we are aware of it, we have a better picture of its effect, impact, and influence. From there, the choice is ours. The Intimate Mind unfolds the possibility of bringing our habitual conditioning into the path of practice and to work toward its transformation.

SUBCONSCIOUS DISTRACTION

We are constantly distracted whether we are awake or asleep. During the waking state we may get distracted as a result of the constant activity of our senses. Depending on our mental and emotional stability this may lead us to feel disturbed and disconnect from the nature of our mind. Even after falling asleep, this disturbed state of our mind may continue and manifest in the form of dreams.

For instance, we may have had a very stressful day or been disturbed by a particular incident. Unless we are able to let go of the feelings with which we respond, our feelings will imprint themselves into our base consciousness*. If we continue to think about the incident, our feelings become stronger. We may believe that as we fall asleep, this will stop. However, our repeated thinking about the incident has made our feelings so strong that they manifest in the form of a dream. When we fall asleep, our sense powers withdraw from the sense fields. This is the first stage of sleep, which is very deep and sound. In the second stage of sleep, when we are totally relaxed, the stronger imprints from the day are released and appear to us as dreams. This happens because they are still active on the subconscious level due to our over-exposure to them during the waking state. The images of our dream may or may not be the same as the situation we experienced during the waking state.

The process of being exposed subconsciously to disturbing images and feelings while we are asleep can cause subtle physical and mental exhaustion. When we dream, we see, hear, feel, taste, and smell exactly as if we were in the waking state, but in actuality it is not happening in that way. In the waking state, the sense fields along with the sense consciousnesses support our mind. During the process of dreaming, they do not support our mind. For example, if we have a dream of a tiger attacking us, we will experience fear and want to get away from the tiger. Our mind is in full function and is asking our body to respond, but we can't. If we were in the waking state, we would have run. So there are two things happening: our mind is asking our body to do something, and our body is forcing itself to follow the mind in our sleep. This causes subtle physical exhaustion.

---

* The base consciousness is like a storehouse in which all our memories and the karmic traces produced by our actions are stored. We can think of these karmic traces as a conditioning that is built up through the course of living life.

If we experience such exhaustion frequently, this has consequences for our health. We become weak, but do not know what
is causing our weakness. We might become depressed as a result
of the subtle exhaustion during our sleep. This is why awareness
is important. If we are able to recognize when we dream that we
are in fact dreaming, this recognition makes it possible for us to
remain free of fear and afflictive emotions.

Unless we are aware of the activity of our mind, we will experience distraction all the time—sleeping and dreaming. Right
now you are reading these lines, but are you completely present
with it? Part of your mind may be passing through your ears and
following the birds chirping outside in the garden. Part of your
mind may be feeling the cold or heat around you. Perhaps the
cushion or chair you are sitting on is not soft enough, giving rise
to the wish for it to be softer. Plans for tomorrow and for later in
the afternoon may be coming in and out of your mind.

Most of the time things happen in this manner. There is always the occurrence of mental diversions. As distraction happens,
it gives birth to habit energy, and then we grasp onto this habitual
conditioning of the mind as real. Consequently, our mind will
operate from this perspective, and we cannot be completely one
with anything.

DISTRACTION AND AWARENESS

When we are distracted, our mind is corrupted. We need to purify our mind so that we can connect with the true nature of
our mind. How can we do this? When we meditate, we can reduce the intensity of distraction. We use antidotes to free our
mind from distraction, and we practice mindfulness of our body,
speech, feelings, and mind. Mindfulness means to bring each and

every thing into the field of our awareness. Mindfulness is an all-pervasive, inclusive, and at the same time penetrative quality of mind. It is the unification of concentration with the quality of awareness that includes everything around us. When we are mindful, we provide a space for everything to unfold in its own way without being disturbed.

Being disturbed is distraction. Through our mindfulness we have the capacity to notice when our mind is getting distracted. Then we can employ our capacity of concentration to free our mind from its disturbed state. Awareness helps us to clearly distinguish whether we are connecting with the source of eternal joy in ourselves or driven by our habit of attachment. Concentration is necessary to remain present during the process of distraction. Without sustained concentration, we will not be able to recognize distraction because our attention will be drawn away before we have really seen what is distracting us.

A state of calmness and tranquility through which the mind abides in itself in oneness is the essence of mindful concentration. What is this oneness? From the perspective of the Intimate Mind, it is being one with Buddha Nature, our inherent nature of awakening. What separates us from Buddha Nature is our distraction. When we practice meditation, we become familiar with the process and nature of distraction. This allows us to recognize the intensity of suffering that we unnecessarily invite through our reaction in the process of distraction. For example, when we are afraid, we may empower our fear so much that we do not see any other possibilities. Empowering our afflictive emotions is the main distraction from the Intimate Mind. We are empowering our fear, desire-attachment, or anger so much that we do not allow our Buddha Nature to manifest at that moment.

There are two kinds of distraction we need to free ourselves from. The first is external distraction. This distraction relates to our environment, our job, our family, society, sounds that we hear, or what is happening in the world. This distraction arises due to our attachment to external sensations and our grasping onto phenomena. The second kind of distraction is internal distraction. This distraction is related to our mind and emotions, and it arises from our conditioning. Both types of distraction can cause us to disconnect from our Buddha nature, although external distraction can only affect us if corresponding conditions are present in our mind. To free ourselves from these two types of distraction, we disconnect from sense agitation and from the afflictive conditioning of our mind. If we can free ourselves from the afflictive conditioning of our mind and from our attachment to phenomena, we will recognize our oneness with Buddha Nature.

The conditioning of our mind that causes distraction consists of the delusion of affliction or emotions and the delusion of intellect. The delusion of affliction is our delusion due to afflictive emotions. The delusion of intellect is our grasping onto views, concepts, and our self-defined reality. This delusion prevents us from realizing the empty nature of all beings. It causes us to make a distinction between the different conditions we experience within the continuum of our consciousness, such as warm and cold, sweet and sour, you and I. In our lives, there is both happiness and sadness. Samsara* and Nirvana exist spontaneously within the continuum of our lives. Due to our delusion of intellect we value and judge our experiences and hold onto preferences and strong views instead of just experiencing them. This is duality. Becoming a Buddha means to realize our freedom from duality.

---

* Samsara is the cycle of suffering that is sustained by the conditioning of afflictive emotions and attachment to views. Nirvana is complete freedom from suffering.

The existence of both happiness and suffering in our life does not mean that we have to let ourselves be affected by both of them. We have the choice to free ourselves from the conditioning that is making us suffer and to create a conditioning that will increase our happiness and peace. This is possible because of our ability to understand what makes us happy and what makes us suffer. If we continue to engage in actions that result in suffering, this is ignorance.

How do we use concentration to free our mind from distraction? Concentration is the opposite of distraction. It is the means by which we can abide in calmness, it is our capacity to rest our mind on one thing at a time. When our mind is disturbed by emotions, we can use concentration together with an antidote to help the mind disconnect from its afflicted state. We shift the mind to a state of love, compassion, or acceptance so that our hatred, anger, or self-judgment can disintegrate by itself. When we are distracted or disturbed, the source of our distraction becomes the object of our mind and attention. In order to free our mind from that, we have to choose a new object of our mind that can help us release the mind from the grasp of distraction. This can be difficult, but it is possible because we have the potential to do it.

To do this, we need to observe our emotions very closely and do our best to become familiar with the relationship of our mind and our emotions, and the cause of our distraction. We notice which emotions we grasp onto and which emotions make us feel disturbed. Once we recognize the cause of our disturbed state of mind, we gather our mind and return it to itself with the help of an antidote. For example, we may have a strong feeling of anger for someone. At that moment, our anger is taking us away from our Buddha Nature. It is taking over our mind, our energy, and our potential. Detaching our mind from the state of anger is not easy because we are the one who is feeling that anger. This is why we need to bring in an external object of mind to help us detach and shift our mind.

What kind of antidote can we use to purify our mind and feelings from anger or hatred? The best antidote for hatred would be a feeling of compassion or love. Yet this may be difficult because the feeling of love is alien to our mind at that moment. In that moment, it will be helpful if we use our object of meditation that we have been practicing with for a long time. Our object of meditation could be our breath, a mantra, an object of visualization such as a deity, or a state of love and compassion. When we practice observing our breath every day, we become familiar with it. We are empowering our breath to be close with our mind. In the same way, we may empower a mantra or deity visualization to be friends with our mind. Becoming friends with the object of our meditation means that we are becoming very connected and familiar with it.

If we practice with our object of meditation every day, in the long run this becomes our strength. Then, when we feel disturbed, we can bring our mind back to the breath, the mantra, or deity because we have made friends with that object. This is much easier than connecting with an object that is not familiar to our mind, which is why we practice meditation or visualization for such a long time. If we spend time with our object of meditation every day for a long time, we have to find a way to become friends with it. Then, when we are in difficulty, our object of meditation is able to help us. If we can do this, we will succeed in purifying our mind.

The essence of the practice of meditation is to bring our mind back home. When we become distracted, we disconnect from the

Intimate Mind, our true nature. By bringing our mind back to the Intimate Mind over and over again, we actualize non-separateness. When we realize that we are not separate from all beings, we actualize our understanding of the interdependent nature of all things. Then we become free from distraction. We become Buddha.

CHAPTER 5

SUBCONSCIOUS ATTACHMENT
TO THE THREE POISONS

SUBCONSCIOUS ATTACHMENT

When we have a perception, the perception is generated both by the external object and by our conditioning. Conditioning can take the form of memories of previous experiences. For instance, when we see a flower, the memory of it is imprinted into our base consciousness. Our life or personality consists of the totality of these small imprints. For someone who hasn't seen a flower before but sees it for the first time, there is no corresponding conditioning that is activated when she sees a flower. In this case, a direct perception can take place, if we are not otherwise distracted by associations that we are making or by our habitual reactions to unknown objects. When we perceive something directly, our mind and the object of our mind unify. If conditioning exists in our mind, our conscious experiences activate different sub-conscious experiences that occur simultaneously with the conscious experience. This subconscious activity does not allow us to perceive the object as it is. In addition, afflicted thoughts based on the three poisons of ignorance, hatred, or desire-attachment will arise due to our holding on to our conditioning. This is subconscious attachment.

When this happens, our mind is divided between two objects without our noticing. One of these objects is the external object of the mind, for instance the flower in the above example. The other is our conditioning, which equally serves as a direct cause of the perception. In the presence of subconscious attachment, a perception which would otherwise lead to a sense of enjoyment will manifest in the form of suffering. This can be prevented if we are aware of the conditioning that is activated subconsciously at the moment of perceiving. This is why in the Bön Buddhist tradition we emphasize maintaining a wholesome state of mind.

IGNORANCE

All forms of life on this planet have the inherent potential of awakened nature. Our human life is so precious because we are given the unique opportunity to be in touch with this awakened nature within ourselves and to reflect the awakened nature of others. Realizing this opportunity is the greatest gift that we can give ourselves. It frees us from our habit of constantly pointing out others' faults and from the suffering that arises as we react to life's situations without seeing their awakened nature.

Ignorance is like the shadow of our awakened nature that constantly follows it. It is the absence of wisdom and the causal seed of all suffering and afflictions. Any kind of affliction of our emotions or mind that stops us from functioning from the true nature of our mind is ignorance, which can take different forms.

There is gross ignorance and subconscious ignorance. If ignorance manifests in a subconscious way, it may affect our good motivation. We may be doing something good for others and feel very motivated to help, but our subconscious ignorance gets in our way without our noticing. Our subconscious ignorance could take the form of doubt in our capacity to accomplish what we intend to do or expectations about how things should work out. The effect of subconscious ignorance is that it does not allow us to reflect on what is going on in our mind. We may think we are doing good and hold on to our expectations or doubts so much that they become our prime objective.

Ignorance loves dark corners. Darkness is its original dwelling place, and its nature is to take everything else into that darkness. In its kingdom of darkness, ignorance fosters afflictive emotions such as desire-attachment and anger. In the Bön Buddhist teachings, ignorance is recognized as the root of all afflictive emotions because it feeds our delusion of emotions and our delusion of intellect. Ignorance obscures the nature of our mind and keeps it from seeing the reality of existence, the impermanence of all compounded phenomena, the lack of an inherent self, and our potential to be free from suffering. Ignorance prevents us from recognizing the causes of suffering in our life. Under the influence of ignorance, we tend to believe that the causes of our suffering exist outside of ourselves. Ignorance does not allow us to turn inward to search for the causes of suffering in our own mind and behavior. This prevents us from transforming the delusion of emotion.

We project judgment onto external objects because of our subconscious attachment to ignorance. Our perception of objects as causes of pleasure and happiness sows a seed of desire-attachment. We produce the craving to have them and own them, although we have no space to keep them in our closet, our refrigerator, our stomach, our house, our bank account, or our mind. We are never content with what we have but feel jealous of the possessions of others. We foster the mind of poverty and engrave a conditioning of stinginess. We might experience temporal happiness when we have access to material possessions. However, subconsciously our possessions become an object of our fear. We expect that our possessions will give us happiness, but our subconscious ignorance turns our relationship with our belongings into one of worry and attachment. If we live our lives based on worry, attachment, and fear, we will be tied with unending suffering.

Ignorance makes us believe fully in the actions we carry out under its influence. In the presence of ignorance there is no wisdom. Without wisdom we are unable to make a clear distinction between wholesome and unwholesome actions of our body, speech, and mind. This causes us to engage in actions that bring suffering into our life and the lives of others.

The very feeling of joy and ease that we may experience by engaging with objects through our senses can also become a condition for afflictive emotions. This could happen with the sense experiences of smell, taste, touch, sound, and sight, or with experiences of the mind, including meditative states or concepts that we become attached to. We all want to be happy and well nourished. In order to maintain happiness, we engage with many activities of wholesome and unwholesome nature in our everyday life. Unwholesome activities have a mentally, emotionally, or physically disturbing effect in our life. Sometimes out of ignorance we make a wrong choice and place ourselves in a difficult situation where we feel stuck.

If we want to act free from the grasp of ignorance, we can question the three essential aspects of benefit, harm, and neutral effect before we engage in an action of body, speech, or mind: If we choose to engage in this action, will it be of benefit for others or for ourselves? Will any harm result from it, or will there be a neutral effect? If we decide not to engage with the action, what will be the benefit, and what will be the harm, or will there be a neutral effect? If we have clarity of mind, we can make a choice that will benefit others and ourselves without harming anyone. In doing this we work toward reducing the power of our habitual conditioning that is governed by ignorance.

We may not be willing to accept our possible contribution toward the arising of a situation or how our actions affect others when we are under the influence of ignorance. Instead, we may tend to blame others. We also tend not to see ourselves when we act out of anger. We only see the object our anger is directed toward. How can we overcome this ignorance? We can learn to pay more attention to how we feel when we see others acting out of afflicted behavior, such as anger. Do that person's actions disturb our state of mind? We can take these observations as a teaching that raises our awareness of the consequences of our actions for others and ourselves.

Due to our holding on to a self-defined concept, we may expect something that does not belong to the nature of reality. When it turns out that reality does not match these expectations, we are unable to look into ourselves and find the cause for this mismatch. We may not realize that our subconscious ignorance is the source of our suffering and that the primary cause for our suffering lies in our own mind. Rather, we blame the external situation for not fitting into our self-defined reality.

In addition to blaming the world outside of us, we may also fight with ourselves and others in order to convince the world of our projected concept of reality. By grasping at our projections and expectations, we make the world around us small. We disconnect from our inherent wisdom that enables us to naturally appreciate and accept each thing as it is.

How can we work with our subconscious ignorance? It is said in the Yum mDo* that there is no sound, taste, touch, smell, or sight. This implies that there is nothing to hold on to. Everything is impermanent and changing all the time. However, impermanence or emptiness does not mean that nothing exists. The taste, touch, smell, and sight we experience in each moment are included within the continuum of our consciousness. If our experience of this moment is unified with our recognition of the impermanent and empty nature of all phenomena, it can become a skillful practice of liberation. If it is unified with the ignorance of desire-attachment or aversion, it becomes an affliction.

It is ignorance that urges us to judge, hold on to, or reject what we experience. This creates a conditioning of desire-attachment or aversion in us. Our conditioning directs our feelings toward the object of our experience. If our feelings are not properly discerned due to a lack of discriminative wisdom, they become the conditioning for craving. Craving narrows down our ability to choose freely and wisely, and thus increases the wandering of our mind. This further stimulates or manipulates our emotions. If we are not aware of the presence of desire-attachment or aversion and their effect on our mind, we may grasp onto the strong emotion that is created by our subconscious ignorance. When we grasp onto this emotion, it becomes the habit of desire-attachment. The habit energy in turn serves as the direct cause of afflicted emotion.

---

* The Yum mDo is a short perfection of wisdom teaching consisting of a dialogue between the compassionate beings Yedki Khui Chung and Tobu Bumsang through the inspiration of Buddha Tonpa Shenrab. The Yum mDo can be regarded as the Bön version of the heart sutra. *Yum* means mother; *mDo* means discourse. The heart sutra is, in many ways, the heart of the Buddhist teachings, and the Yum mDo is the heart of the teachings of the Bön Buddha Tonpa Shenrab.

Wholesome habits arise in the same way. Here, the conditioning has the form of our aspiration to engage in wholesome actions and to refrain from actions that create suffering. If the conditioning is free of ignorance, its result can be wholesome and reduce our suffering. If it is motivated by ignorance, it will increase our suffering in the form of afflictive emotions. If our mind, feelings, and body support our wholesome intention and wholesome action, this can be our greatest strength to liberate ourselves.

THE THREEFOLD IGNORANCE

The Ignorance of Doubt

Doubt, strong views, and pride are expressions of our ignorance. The nature of our mind is free from doubt. When we have doubts, we have disconnected from the nature of the mind. The nature of the mind is accompanied by wisdom. The doubting mind is characterized by the afflictions of judgment, ignorance, self-centeredness, and fear. If we are experiencing doubt, we need to ask: What makes me doubt? What is it that takes me to a space where doubt takes over my mind?

Doubt is subconscious attachment to the desire realm. We have ideas about how things should be, how others should behave and live, how the teachings should be, or where we should be with our life and our practice. As we hold on to that, our mind gets split into doubt and expectations. We create a separation between the world around us and ourselves.

For instance, when we listen to our loved one, we may begin to feel that she is hiding something and not being truthful with us, instead of trusting and receiving her words completely. We need to ask ourselves why we are doing this. What is the cause that gives rise to the doubt in our mind? Sometimes we have a strong attachment to our past experience, for instance of a situation where someone has not been truthful with us. That situation has nothing to do with our present situation, but our subconscious attachment to it is so strong that it impairs our cognitive capacity to perceive the reality of the present moment. Because of the conditioning imprinted on our body and mind, we have become subconsciously attached to fear. Our fear gives birth to doubt, and Samsara continues. Samsara is the process of cyclic continuum, the continuum of ignorance, doubt, desire-attachment, and the resulting afflictive actions.

When we develop the wish to free others and ourselves from suffering, we may experience difficulties and doubt. When our actions to help others fail, or when suffering continues to be present in us, we may not have the heart to accept this without judgment and without losing our confidence. Instead we judge ourselves. This makes us unable to act in the way we wish. We create the obscuration of doubt and judgment based on our fear. We also project this judgment onto others, causing ourselves to lose the connection of love, trust, and respect.

Questioning oneself is not always harmful. When our questioning has a quality of acknowledgement and acceptance, it can be an expression of continuous learning that is characterized by wisdom. In this case, our questioning is rooted in self-care and compassion and does not involve self-judgment or discouragement. This means that we are not using doubt to prevent our awakening. Part of the self-care that leads to our questioning is the motivation to wake up. This gives us the desire to investigate and find out the truth. It is part of the thought that turns the mind toward its essence. On the other hand, if we have doubt based on fear or an unwholesome attitude, we experience suffering. We may not notice this suffering because of its subtle nature, and because we are preoccupied with the doubt. In this case, the suffering we experience in the process of doubting becomes imprinted into our base consciousness. Later on, this imprint will be activated under a constructive condition and we will feel its effect.

How can we work with doubt? First, we have to realize that doubt is part of our mind. We cannot end doubt, but we can reduce the suffering that accompanies it. Whatever practice we do, a major part of working toward awakening is to reduce the pain and suffering that arise from our doubts and to do our best not to solidify doubt into a habit that becomes a subconscious addiction. Sometimes, circumstances pressure us into believing others are judging us. We then feel we are not capable or good enough. We doubt our capacity and lose our confidence. Our practice is to give space to others' judgment and use it as a tool to know ourselves better. If we let another's judgment carry us away, it will not help us, but rather take away our hope and strength and lead us into suffering. But if we look deeply into the nature of reality, we may be able to benefit from another's criticism. We have the potential to be free and strong. Sometimes we don't know ourselves because we are too caught up in our self-centeredness to see our shadow. It is a great gift that others may still see our weaknesses and point them out to us. It is our practice to recognize this gift, rather than to become defensive and feel discouraged when somebody criticizes us.

When we allow ourselves to be affected by another's judgment, often we feel what will help us most is the warm acceptance that a close loved one can give us. If we have the courage to look deeply into ourselves without feeling overwhelmed by judgment or denial, we can learn to give this kind of unconditional acceptance to ourselves. Our own acceptance of ourselves and others is one of the strongest antidotes to doubt.

The Ignorance of Pride

Pride is subconscious insecurity. Our inability to recognize this is ignorance. Sometimes our subconscious attachment to pride waters the seeds of egotistic self-centeredness. When self-centeredness takes over our consciousness, it puts an end to continuous learning. It blinds us with the wall of dualism, separating the nature of our mind from the external reality of phenomena. We hold onto this self-identity and to a dualistic view of others and ourselves. Our subconscious attachment to pride makes us perceive ourselves as more intelligent, wealthier, more beautiful, or more realized than others. Under the influence of pride we cannot learn from others. Pride obscures our innate wisdom and makes us unable to appreciate or bear witness to the nurturing qualities of others.

Under the influence of pride we are like a clay jar with a closed lid. No matter what we or others try to put into the jar, nothing will enter it. In the same way, pride acts as a lid to the openness of our heart and mind. The true nature of phenomena is interdependence. There is so much to learn from others and to be grateful for. Being open to continuous learning will help us reduce our subconscious insecurity. It will enable us to learn from others and to let go of preoccupying concepts and ideas that cause separation and suffering.

It is our fear of suffering that makes us insecure. We may feel the need to proceed on our path, or to receive appreciation for our perceived special qualities because of a subconscious belief that this will protect us from suffering. To overcome our attachment to pride and our insecurity, we need to look at the world with less judgment and with acceptance for our suffering. If we can do this, we will be much less affected by fear, and we will give no fear to others.

Often we put ourselves in an insecure state of being based on the judgment that results from our pride. We become the victim of jealousy. For instance, if we look at those whom we perceive to be in a better position than ourselves, this can be overwhelming and make us insecure. Instead of allowing ourselves to become overwhelmed, we can stop and look with compassion at those who are in a less fortunate situation than ourselves and who need our help. Through our compassion we cultivate a heart of self-acceptance and the mind of continuous learning. If we do this, we will realize the essence of inter-being. Inter-being is the reality of you and me helping each other. When I am weak, ugly, and suffering, will you help me to be strong, beautiful, and free of pain? Inter-being is the practice of helping each other without judgment and without preconceived ideas about what the other needs based on our own identity. This practice of inter-being reduces the constant activation of our subconscious insecurity, and it frees us from the suffering caused by the confining lid of pride.

The Ignorance of Views

Right views or wrong views—
this is a creation of our own mind.
Attachment to right view,
aversion to wrong view
is a creation of our own mind.
Holding on
to the duality of concepts
is a great delusion of ignorance.

The spiritual and intellectual traditions of this world each have their own practices and views. Every religion has its view. Scientists, economists, artists, and shamans each have their views. These views are a great treasure. We are both the beneficiaries and protectors of these views. However, due to our subconscious ignorance, our wish to protect our own view may prevent us from acknowledging and appreciating the great gift of others' views so that we cannot benefit from the wisdom of others. We may think that we are Bön Buddhists and that the view of this tradition is the best view of all. This may be true based on our experience and based on how our tradition has helped us bring positive changes into our life. However, while the Bön Buddhist view is a very good view, other spiritual traditions such as Christianity, Hinduism, Islam, Judaism, or Sikh have benefited numberless beings in their own way throughout space and time. More importantly, if we hold on to the view from which we are trying to learn, we prevent ourselves from being fully transformed by it. If we are afraid rather than open, transformation cannot take place.

As individuals, we also have an individual view with wholesome and unwholesome aspects. If we are attached to the unwholesome aspects of our view, our view becomes like a dark cloud that obscures the sun. Then, our view can isolate us from the rest of the world. The wholesome aspects of our view may protect us from misfortunes and open the door to many possibilities, but if we are obsessed with our view and our perspective, we narrow our vast innate potential of goodness that can radiate in every moment of our life. We create a wall of self-centered ego that prevents us from receiving the nurturing qualities of others. Under the strong influence of our view we may not be able to give others the space to be who they are. Over time, our attachment to our view can develop into a subconscious form of ego. It is better to have no view at all than to have a view that is rooted in egotistic self-centeredness.

Our subconscious attachment to our view can blind us instead of creating the clear vision of awareness and a deeper understanding of reality. Rigidly holding on to a specific idea, concept, or belief narrows down the space that is available for our mind and heart to be more open and accepting. The unification of the openness of our mind and the openness of our heart is the essence of equanimity. Without openness and acceptance, equanimity cannot shine forth. If equanimity stays merely in our mind as a thought or idea, equanimity itself also becomes a view. True equanimity includes in its nature all views and phenomena. It puts an end to the duality of the thinking mind.

Our attachment to our view puts us in a box. The insecurity that arises from fear and shame prevents us from coming out of that box. Without being aware of this, we may judge ourselves and the world according to the view we are holding on to. Our view may have great potential to be helpful, but if we do not understand its functioning and purpose, we cannot live up to its deeper meaning. Beyond this we may end up misusing our view to create war, suffering, and pain. This may happen both with a view of spiritual practice and a practical view of individual development and livelihood. Our view has to have a truly wholesome intention at its base, such as the wish to help others and to develop true kindness. When our view is based on this wish, it will contribute to our own development and to the beauty of this world. Then it can be like the sun which illuminates the darkness and gives warmth to all without discrimination.

HATRED AND ANGER

Anger or hatred is one of the three main afflictions that create Samsara, the ongoing cycle of suffering in our life. When we feel hatred or anger toward someone, our mind is afflicted. Depending on how we respond to the initial moment when something happens that makes us angry, there are two possibilities: We may liberate the anger at that very moment, or we could become affected by it. If we hold on to anger toward someone, it perpetuates. For instance we may start thinking about how he or she may harm us now or in the future, and this thought may dominate our mind and heart.

When anger takes hold of our mind, it also afflicts our sense consciousnesses. When anger passes through our eyes, we see everything as fearful and ugly. When anger afflicts our ear consciousness, we will hear whatever the other person says as disturbing or meaningless. When anger afflicts our speech, we may speak in a way that harms others, even with people we do not really want to harm. When anger affects our body, we lose control of our actions and may physically harm others or ourselves. It is important to recognize that anger is a creation of our mind and its nature is empty. This understanding helps us stop anger from afflicting our feelings and our sense perceptions. If we can reduce or stop the arising of anger, this will also prevent the development of karmic conditions that will serve as causes for our anger in the future.

Sometimes we encounter a situation that puts us in a state of helplessness and confusion. Anger loves taking advantage of our helplessness and confusion. When we are angry, we are no longer able to reflect calmly on whether our response to a situation is suitable or helpful. For instance, there are situations when a large part of the population feels betrayed by government in the face of corruption, war, or an inability to conduct reforms. There may be a very strong feeling of disagreement with the actions taken by government. This puts the individual into a state of deep helplessness that can stimulate a lot of anger. I remember people expressing such feelings at the beginning of the American war on Iraq. My own feeling is that it does not help me or anyone else if I become angry with myself because of my helplessness or with someone else because of his or her actions. My getting angry at the other person is not going to help him or her change. Rather, it is only causing pain, suffering, and depression in my life.

If a whole country blames their politicians and everybody is angry with them, this generates a strong level of anger in the entire country. This does not leave much space for the compassion and wisdom that are needed to find and establish a better course of action. When we are angry, instead of touching others with our compassion and wisdom, we may end up affecting innocent people like our family and friends with our anger. Our anger may affect them so that they also begin to experience anger. This is an example of how our subconscious attachment to anger can result in a chain reaction. If we instead send a prayer of love and compassion toward our politicians, a natural healing might occur. When we pray, we connect with our love and compassion. Entering into that space of mind protects us from becoming a victim of anger, and it stops our anger from spreading. On the other hand, if we are angry with another person, the negative and chaotic energy in that person may increase, and this will contribute to their anger and toward actions based on anger.

According to the Bön teachings on healing energy, anger not only disturbs our mind but also reduces the strength of our liver. Anger stimulates the liver cells and this creates an excess of energy in the liver. How does the excess of energy in the liver cause mental or emotional disturbance? When there is an excess of energy in the liver, it puts pressure on the stomach. This stimulates the spleen. Affecting the spleen means affecting the earth element. When the earth element is disturbed, it gives rise to worries, fear, and mental and emotional insecurity. Under the effect of anger, our blood pressure gets high. This puts pressure on our brain, making us unstable and nervous.

When we are affected by anger, how can we turn our mind to forgiveness? To work with our anger, it is essential that we strengthen our stability and our awareness. Mental and emotional stability, gratitude, and awareness are the key practices to reduce the agony of anger. If milk boils over, it will spill out of the container and make a mess. In the same way when we are angry, it will heat us up. It will flow out of us, affect others, and damage ourselves. We have become like the pot of boiling milk that overflows. What should we do in this case? If milk is boiling over, we can transfer it into a bigger pot or turn off the fire underneath it. If we can return to our stability, this is like turning off the fire of our emotions. And like milk being transferred to a bigger pot, with self-awareness it becomes possible to give space to our emotions and our state of mind without being affected by them.

The first thing we need to do when we are under the control of anger is to fully recognize that we are angry. We do this without giving rise to any further reaction in the form of self-judgment, blame, or fear. When we recognize how we feel, this gives us the strength and awareness we need to acknowledge and accept the state of our being. This recognition allows us to witness the state of our being and its consequences, and to apply an antidote to our anger. Antidotes shift the mind from an afflicted state to a positive state. Forgiveness, love, compassion, and gratitude are powerful antidotes to anger. When we are angry, the first person we need to forgive is ourselves. Being in a state of anger is suffering, whether we are angry with others or with ourselves. We need to forgive ourselves for not being a Buddha at that moment. Forgiving ourselves unifies our heart and mind and frees our energy from the constant need to work against or justify how we are feeling. Once we have forgiven ourselves, forgiving another person or a situation becomes much easier.

In working with our anger, we have to be patient. This is not easy, as patience may not manifest by itself. We have to help our mind, either by just observing our anger and letting it go, or by looking into the nature of anger. Anger is due to certain causes, and it is impermanent; it will not stay with us. If we hold on to feelings of hatred, either for ourselves or others, then we hinder the revelation of impermanence. If we truly wish to reduce the pain and suffering we experience because of anger, we need to forgive. Focusing on what someone has done to disturb us will hinder our potential to forgive. We need to open our mind and heart to acknowledge that the other person is influenced by her or his imperfection and afflictions. Then our heart and mind can be touched by the other's suffering of imperfection and affliction rather than by her or his actions. This will help us to recognize the other's suffering and to generate unconditional compassion and forgiveness.

DESIRE AND SELF-AWARENESS

It was the month of September in Humla, Nepal, a few months before I left for India to undergo monastic training at Menri monastery. I was six years old. One fine late morning the whole village was gathering for a meeting. My grandfather, who was head of the village, was facilitating the council. I was sitting in his lap. Someone came up and offered a slice of apple to my grandfather. My grandfather took a bite and gave the rest to me. I looked at it and smelled it. It looked good and smelled good too. When I ate it, it tasted so good because it was very sweet. Humla is one of the most remote places in Western Nepal. Apples were very uncommon as I was growing up. The sweet taste of the apple stayed with me. I was happy because I really enjoyed it.

At that very moment one of the elders said, "This apple tastes really good. Where is it from?"

Paljor brother replied, "It is from my brother-in-law in the next village. They have two trees."

Slowly, my mind began to grasp onto the sweetness of the apple, and this very grasping produced a simple thought which eventually began to merge with desire. My feeling was that I wanted to have more of those apples. At that time it was just in my mind. Later my over-exposure to this thought overtook my body and speech as well. By the next morning the apple had become my whole body, speech, and mind.

Early afternoon the next day, I was hunting for my friend who could go with me to the next village to steal apples. I did not find any of my friends around. So I decided to go back home. As I was walking up toward my house, my neighbor's door opened. There I saw Sonam, my friend. He was rather slow and gentle— very different from me who could not easily stay in one place and had to be doing something all the time. So, gently I unfolded the supreme idea to him. I was a bit hesitant, feeling that he might not like my idea of stealing apples from the next village. I was struggling with the fear of rejection. Somehow I was able to convince him of the great taste of the apples.

So we set off. The sun was above the mountains. We walked down by the bushes in the millet field with fear and excitement, attempting to keep people from seeing us. There wasn't anybody around. We were both hiding in the millet field. We finally reached the village. I knew exactly where the house was because one could see the whole village from my own village above. Soon the sun was gone and it was getting dark. People were still on their roofs, talking to each other. We waited. We were afraid, not only of being caught, but also because we had heard some humorous and maybe some serious rumors of ghosts. I was terrified. We waited and waited.

Finally everyone went inside their houses, so we walked closer to the house where we saw two big trees with hundreds of apples that were deep red in color. Seeing the apples I disconnected from the terror of ghosts. We entered into the garden through the fence. We slowed down. I was standing right under a huge apple tree. Unfortunately I was little and all the red apples were on the far top of the tree. The apples closer to the ground were all green. So I asked my friend to stay under the tree while I climbed up. My desire brought me there. And there I was in the tree.

It did not end there. It continued as the desire merged with my attachment to the color of the apples and this took me further and further, reaching for the bright red apples on the top—to the point where the branch of the apple tree was no longer able to hold my weight and broke. I fell to the ground.

On hearing the sound of the breaking branch the family rushed out of the house, shouting and yelling, "Someone is stealing the apples!"

I ran. Meanwhile I realized that I wasn't running, actually, I was falling. Falling from the top of the next house whose roof was attached to the field where the apple tree was. When I hit the ground, all I could see was stars oozing out of my head, through my eyes. Unfortunately I did not get much time to take care of myself because I had actually fallen into the main entrance door of the apple-owner.

I heard someone shouting, "Here he is! Come down!"

They chased after me. I was a fast runner. As I was growing up I used to run a lot with my friends, but here it seemed impossible to run in front of two adults so I decided to run up the hill into the millet field rather than running straight. I was nervous. I was afraid. All I could think of was how to escape, and this very thought gave birth to another thought in the form of an idea of throwing stones at my pursuers as I was a little bit higher up at the hill. As I started to throw stones at them, they ran further down to avoid the stones.

Once the men had given up chasing me, I slowly headed toward my village. It was totally dark now. I could hear the jackal crying. I was no longer afraid of people because they were not chasing me anymore, and yet I was losing my strength as I walked uphill through the dark. Once again my base consciousness released its grip and the memory of ghost stories told by my grandmother and other people from the village slowly overtook my whole being. At the same time I could hear the sharp sound of crying coming closer to me. I was so afraid that I could not turn and look back or pay attention. I just kept moving uphill. I could still hear the sound but it was now a little bit further away from me. Yet the sound was moving parallel to me.

I felt much better as I reached my village. There were some people near the walkway. To avoid them I took another path to my home. There I ran into Sonam, my partner in the apple-quest. He was sobbing. He was naked. I asked him what had happened to his clothes.

At first he was not ready to tell me. Then with mumble he said, "They took my clothes!"

I asked, "Who they?"

He replied, "They caught me and took away my clothes."

We discussed what to do. We were both so afraid that my friend's family would beat him for losing his clothes. So I decided to take him into my house. As I entered the main entrance gate of my courtyard something happened to me. I don't know why—I burst out crying. I cried so loud that my friend was telling me to stop, as otherwise people would hear me. He held my hand and we sat down for a few more minutes. As I began to feel better I had another idea. So I took him inside my house.

In Humla, in particular in the Nyimba valley, the houses have three stories. On the ground floor are the stable rooms where animals are kept. The kitchen, dining room, and living space are on the second floor. On the third floor are bedrooms, the prayer and meditation hall, and a few other rooms for storage. I took my friend to the little room where we keep the baby goats and yaks. I told him to stay there while I went up and brought food and clothes. I cleaned my face and walked into the kitchen. I could hear my sister calling loudly for me from the roof of my house. My grandmother went out and told my sister that I was back home.

Everyone in the family started eating. I told them that I was going to sleep. I took my plate and a sheep's skin-blanket to my friend. It was very dark, as we don't have electricity in Humla. We got into the blanket and ate the food. I remembered that I had put one apple in my pocket. Luckily it was still there. I took it out and we ate it in the dark, not knowing whether it was red or green. The taste was very good. It was a brief moment, yet it taught me a great lesson. Now looking back into that brief moment of my life, part of me feels like laughing, and at the same time like crying.

In the monastery, there are different precepts that are observed by the monks and nuns. These precepts are designed to protect the individual from certain mental factors that are accompanied by an unwholesome attitude that could destroy everything. With one simple thought impairing our sense fields, we can become a victim of that thought and of the resulting afflictive emotions. The precepts and meditation practice are designed so we can always stay connected with our basic human goodness. Yet, sometimes within the practice of these precepts, we forget our natural, inherent potential to be good, and become dependent on them, so that we are no longer able to do well without them. Then the precepts become like a wall that confines our potential for inherent goodness.

Life in the monastery is easy in the sense that everybody lives by the same precepts and the same motivation and aspiration and carries out the same practice every day. It is impossible and inappropriate for everybody to become monks and nuns and live in the monastery. The majority of us are living our everyday lives in the world. There are no precepts like monks and nuns have, and it would be impossible to create precepts or rules that would apply to each individual. Of course we have law enforcement, but its reach is limited. Maybe this is because we are so obsessed with the fantasies of our self-defined freedom. It depends upon us, upon each individual, to discover how we can live in harmony, how we can bring peace into our lives and onto this planet without everybody following the same precepts or regulations.

It is not just precepts that protect us from ill intention. Ultimately, it is our innate wisdom of self-awareness that protects us from falling into the field of distraction. We need to understand the process through which distraction occurs and leads to grasping and afflicted emotions in the absence of self-awareness. When we understand this process, we will have faith in the power of self-awareness.

It is our natural human potential to be self-aware. When we are self-aware, we bring our mind, heart, and actions into harmony with the world. Each of our actions can affect the present moment as it is experienced by ourselves and others. In the presence of self-awareness, we are no longer dominated by the subconscious attachment of ignorance or by desire-attachment. We do not think only of ourselves and our attachments but also of other beings who share this moment with us. Once we understand the power of self-awareness and the necessity for it, we will learn to watch the reactions in our mind in each moment. We can learn not to let subconscious grasping or feelings of aversion dominate our mind and separate us from each moment.

DESIRE-ATTACHMENT

Desire that is free from attachment is a quality of the nature of the mind. It can open our heart and mind and help us connect with everything around us. It can be a causal seed for loving kindness, compassion, joy, and equanimity. If we look deeply into the aspiration of the Intimate Mind, to help all beings be free from pain and suffering, we will find an aspect of desire in it. This desire is in its purest form, free from attachment. If we are motivated by the pure wish to become a compassionate being, we aspire to cultivate wholesome qualities, and we take hold of disturbed feelings and conditions that constantly haunt our inner strength and peace with the intention to eliminate them. This quality of our mind allows us to open our heart, and it gives us the strength to move forward without becoming buried in the chaos of despair, fear, or disappointment.

Desire has the potential of both wholesome and unwholesome nature. Desire itself may not necessarily be suffering, but it becomes suffering when it controls our mind and body, when it destroys our innate strength and freedom of choice, and when it disconnects us from the wisdom of acceptance and clarity. It is not desire that stimulates our mind and feelings; it is our conditioning of subconscious attachment that creates and invites desire and grasping into action and makes them stronger. We make our desires so real that we begin to believe they are truly needs.

If the pure state of the desire of a wholesome motivation is mixed with attachment, it becomes expectation. Expectation is subconscious attachment. Subconscious attachment reflects our ignorance, and it is a causal seed of suffering and pain in our life. It opens the door for the conditioning of addictive needs that are based on desire-attachment.

Desire-attachment can develop out of the grasping of the mind onto an object such as an experience of the senses, a concept, a state of mind, a feeling, or a situation. Grasping is not a problem by itself. What is problematic is our inability to recognize our grasping. When the mind grasps onto an object, we are no longer able to see, acknowledge, and accept the impermanent nature of all things. We want our object of desire to remain exactly as it is. When we recognize our grasping, we have a choice to grasp or not to grasp. This frees us to acknowledge and accept the true nature of impermanence. Everything changes. Not accepting this truth by holding onto a particular feeling, experience, or external condition puts us in a vulnerable state of mind and emotions. This becomes a favorable condition for grasping to manifest in the form of desire-attachment, and this leads us into suffering and pain.

If we investigate thoroughly, we may find that it is we ourselves who create the conditions for encountering situations, and it is we who experience the consequences. When we believe in these situations and follow them, we give rise to grasping and craving. Grasping can occur either through direct contact of the senses with an object, or through grasping without sensual contact. Either way, our grasping and the object we grasp play the role of cause and effect. Grasping through sensual contact has a more limited effect than grasping without sensual contact, because we grasp without the support of an object. Grasping without the support of an object is more subjective and can be more manipulative in its disturbing nature.

We may think that we are born with habitual conditioning such as addiction. It is possible that part of it is due to a genetic disposition, yet the larger role is played by our lack of awareness and stability which then allows us to be carried away by our conditioning. In the absence of awareness and stability of mind, our conditioning of desire-attachment stimulates our emotions. This activates an exaggerated concept of a certain object, feeling, or perception and a strong desire for it. This desire is based on our previous experience of the satisfaction and comfort we have derived from the object.

Desire-attachment can obscure and take over not only our mind and consciousness, but also our sense fields. Under the strong influence of desire-attachment, the true essence of our sense powers is corrupted. This corruption occurs through the mixing of our sense powers with ignorance. When our sense powers are mixed with ignorance, our awareness is distorted and no longer conforms to the reality of the sense objects we encounter, but reveals the conditioning imposed by desire-attachment. Instead of seeing an object as it is, our experience is dominated by our conditioning of desire-attachment.

If we desire something we cannot have, and we are able to acknowledge this without being distracted from the natural state of our mind, that is wisdom. If we do not have this acceptance, that is ignorance. Our inability to recognize that it is okay not to receive what we want affects our behavior, our emotions, and our mind. We feel insecure, angry, or jealous, and we forget who we really are. Instead, we become a weapon of desire-attachment and its afflictions. Then we are being used against ourselves in an uncompassionate, unskillful, and unwholesome way, and we hurt others and ourselves.

DESIRE AND THE NATURE OF THE MIND

If desire is mixed with attachment, the resulting emotion is of afflicted nature and leads us into emotional chaos and mental instability. How does desire turn into its destructive form of desire-attachment? What are the causes that turn desire into desire-attachment and emotions into afflicted emotions?

Desire-attachment emerges when the functions of our six senses* operate in the absence of self-awareness, wisdom of cognition, and mental stability. Self-awareness means knowing ourselves. It enables us to know how we are affected. The wisdom of cognition enables us to catch what we are doing with the sharp precision of a falcon catching its prey. Inner stability is necessary to prevent us from becoming distracted or carried away by our feelings and by external sense objects. When we are unstable, our desire has more control over us, and the connection we make with objects will be based on our desire-attachment. Under the influence of desire-attachment we believe that the objects we encounter are real and truly exist out there. If we have this belief, we let the situation affect us.

In our life we see, hear, and touch many things. Some are beautiful and some are not. Our sense perceptions and the resulting emotions are like clouds in the sky that disappear only momentarily. A sense perception that is encountered without the presence of self-awareness will create an imprint in our conscious-

---

* In Bön and Buddhism, our six senses are sight, sound, smell, taste, touch, and the mind.

ness, and its effects will stay with us. If we have self-awareness, we have a choice whether to hold on to it or to let it go. Being affected by a sense perception can take place on a conscious, subconscious, or unconscious level. Perceptions and emotions that remain on the subconscious or unconscious level may seem to have disappeared, but they have only moved outside the field of our awareness. They remain active on the subconscious or unconscious level of our mind where they serve as condition for desire-attachment or aversion.

When a perception or emotion remains active within us, it may manifest in different forms through the imprints it has created. Afflictive reactions can manifest as addictive need, depression, fear, anger, or different levels of mental disturbance. These effects are hard to observe in the absence of self-awareness and wisdom of cognition. If we live in the present moment with full awareness and clarity, we can reduce the imprint of karmic traces and their effect on our emotions and behavior. For instance, if we lie in order to escape from a situation without being aware of this, our willingness to lie and the associated emotions will become imprinted into our mind. If we encounter another situation from which we want to escape, the existing karmic trace related to lying may surface and cause us to lie again.

In the presence of awareness, wisdom of cognition, and stability, the experiences we encounter through our senses may give us strength and happiness. When we see a flower, we have a perception of a flower. We can respond to this perception in different ways. The sense perception of the flower as beautiful or ugly is created by our thinking mind. Any perception based on the thinking mind can be of a distracting nature, such as a feeling that stimulates desire-attachment or a feeling that relives past experiences. If the perception is discerned with wisdom of cognition, it can be a source of joy. Then we can use it to unify with our capacity of eternal joy at that moment. Without wisdom of cognition we cannot recognize how we are responding and whether we are responding out of the conditioning of attachment, aversion, or judgment.

We also need inner stability to provide a firm ground for our wisdom of cognition so that we are not distracted by our deep-seated conditioning of desire-attachment before our wisdom of cognition can make a choice. In the absence of stability, desire-attachment may control our state of joy and happiness. This can condition us to want more of a particular experience or to want to suppress it. This conditioning can give rise to grasping, which can take away our willpower and peace of mind. Then we become a slave of the experience encountered. We may see the pain, dishonesty, and unwholesomeness of this experience, but feel that we have no other choice. In this case, our desire-attachment and our subconscious ignorance take advantage of our conditioning.

When stability is present, it turns our heart and mind to the experience of that moment so that we can stay with it and also fully let go of it. This allows us to just feel the experience of the moment and to be with it while it is present. We unify our sense perception with emptiness. Awareness can take us to the essence of the perception of that moment, and wisdom of cognition allows us to appreciate it. It enables us to make a clear choice guided by self-awareness, so that our experience of that moment is not directed toward a disturbed state of mind but toward engagement with an undistracted and joyful state of mind.

CHAPTER 6

OUR ADDICTION TO FEAR

Dropping our addiction to fear
we recognize
that fear is not separate
from the nature of our mind.

Often we are not aware of fear's presence in us. We are afraid of many things in our life but do not recognize this because our fears may be subconscious and take the form of different afflictive emotions. We are worried, and we experience stress, pride, or jealousy, which are subtle forms of fear. Most of our fears are based on self-judgment. When we judge ourselves or others, the subtle fear that has caused our judgment is imprinted onto our consciousness. Through our repeated exposure to judgment and afflictive emotions, the conditioning for fear strengthens. This conditioning manifests as a need to feel fear, so that when we encounter a similar situation, we tend to respond again with fear. Thus, fear becomes an addiction. When fear becomes an addiction, we fall under its power, and we are always insecure or afraid.

From the viewpoint of the Intimate Mind, fear is not separate from the nature of our mind. The nature of the mind is empty. This is also true for feelings, including fear. Fear is simply a projection of the mind. Its nature cannot be different from the nature of the mind, which is emptiness. If we recognize the empty nature of fear when it arises, it will dissolve by itself. No karmic traces will be collected, and no suffering will follow. When we have this understanding, we are neither judging nor holding on to our fear.

Living with fear is suffering; judging our fear or holding on to it is ignorance. These secondary emotions with which we respond to fear can be very powerful. Judgment takes us into a state of mind where we make a situation more fearful because we separate the fear from its empty nature. Our subconscious judgment turns our fear into something powerful. This makes us doubt our capacity to transform our feelings and respond in a positive way. We become the victim of that fearful state of mind. Since fear is not separate from the nature of our mind, it is not necessary to respond to fear by turning it into a powerful enemy. It is because of our addiction to fear that we become part of the process of fear.

Fear disrupts the natural flow of energy in our body and in the stream of consciousness that is necessary in order for our true nature of love, openness, and compassion to manifest. This is how we lose our natural potential and the strength that would hold us in a stable state. When we fear something and fail to realize that this fear is not separate from the natural state of our mind, we invite fear into our life. The very moment fear arises, we have a choice to be afraid or not to be afraid. When we recognize that the fear is not separate from the nature of our mind, we provide a space for the fear to dissolve. If we do not realize this, we are affected by fear and only strengthen it.

When our fear becomes strong, it dominates our whole consciousness and weakens our senses' ability to function. There is a subtle attachment to fear beneath how we think, see, or hear. We operate from that underlying fear. What we see and experience—what we feel in response to any object—will be colored by that subtle fear. At this point, the information collected by our senses can no longer merge with the true nature of the mind to allow us to perceive directly. If our perception merges with the conditioning of fear held in our consciousness, we can no longer perceive the actual nature of the sensory object of that moment; we perceive everything as fearful based on our conditioning.

ELEMENTS OF FEAR

When we look deeply into the nature of fear and its relationship with the object of fear, we will see that the afflicted mind consciousness* is the principal causal contributor to the arising of fear. The afflicted mind consciousness is the mind that feeds on afflictive emotions. There are also secondary contributors to the arising of fear: imbalances in the five elements of earth, water, fire, air, and space; imbalances in our organs; or imbalances in our six senses and sense consciousnesses. There is a subtle emotion that links our physical body to the arising of fear. If the afflicted mind consciousness did not exist, would we still experience fear? To perceive fear, the afflicted mind consciousness has to be present. We would not be able to experience fear without it.

---

* There are eight consciousnesses: the consciousness of the eye, ear, nose, tongue, body, and mind; the afflicted or deluded mind consciousness; and the base consciousness in which karmic traces are stored.

From the perspective of the Bön healing practice of the elements, the five elements, five major organs, five senses, and five major chakras or energy centers correspond to different afflictive emotions and to the five wisdom qualities. The five major organs are the spleen, kidneys, liver, lungs, and heart. Among these, the kidneys together with the water element are directly connected to fear. If the energy of the kidneys is imbalanced, it holds fear and gives it space to grow. When we experience constant fear, the kidneys lose their strength. The functioning and health of the kidneys is determined by the balance of the water element in us. When the water element in our body is in balance, we feel less fear. Since our kidneys are controlled by the water element, the nature of fear can be fluid and easy to influence.

What causes imbalances in the water element in us? The elements in us are all interrelated. When the earth element is imbalanced by anger, this imbalance stimulates the liver cells, giving rise to fire energy. Then our kidneys have to produce more water. An excess of fire energy also puts pressure on the spleen, the major organ corresponding to the earth element. This results in an imbalance in the earth element. On the emotional level, this imbalance contributes to the arising of worry and anxiety, which in turn serves as a causal seed of fear. On the physical and energetic level, the earth needs water to regenerate its energy and heal itself. It cannot itself produce water. This puts pressure on the water element and its corresponding major organ, the kidneys. The absorption or over-absorption of energy from the kidneys by the earth element can stimulate the kidneys to produce more energy, or it can damage them. When the kidneys become weak, we can become victims of fear. When fear occupies the space around our heart, we feel agitated, impatient, or angry. This puts pressure on our lungs, causing an imbalance in the air element. This results in sadness or depression in our life.

Another organ that contributes to the arising of fear is the bladder, which is related to the kidneys. The bladder stimulates desire-attachment in us. How does desire-attachment lead to fear? Our strong attachment to people, possessions, or our own life makes us unable to let go. This gives birth to fear of loss or fear of being unable to support our livelihood, fear of change and un-certainty, and fear of death or destruction. In this way we bind ourselves with the fear of suffering.

Our ears and the sense of hearing are a secondary contribu-tor to the arising of fear. Hearing can produce a direct perception of fear. If we walk in the dark and hear a sudden sound coming out of the bush, we are afraid. If we hear about violence, war, an epidemic, or a natural disaster, we experience fear. When we hear somebody shouting, this can cause fear. Even when somebody disagrees with or gossips about us, this can cause feelings of fear in us. The TV and newspaper media every day bring the news. Just hearing the news every day—how many of us lose our peace of mind by letting them affect us and produce a sense of fear? And how many of us remain stable and unaffected?

Constantly putting ourselves into situations where we feel fear, we may become a fertile ground for fear to germinate. The more we are exposed to fear, the more inclined we are to turn our mind toward fear instead of connecting with our innate wis-dom. This weakens our ability to be unafraid and takes away our strength. Our innate wisdom can give us the strength to be stable, calm, and joyful; it is our potential to approach each situation with skill, confidence, and understanding. Through our habit of judging and worrying, we disconnect from this wisdom.

Our sense of hearing also contributes to the development of fear through our memories. Memories of something we have heard and that has caused fear in us become imprinted into our consciousness and can continue to cause us to be afraid. For example, when sitting quietly, we may find ourselves starting to think about death or an incident that threatened us, and find fear arising in us. Part of this fear arises from what we have heard about the pain and insecurity experienced at the moment of death.

We may think that our sense of sight can also produce fear. What happens when we perceive an object that we could be afraid of with our eyes? For instance, when we look at a tiger, our eyes see only the tiger's physical appearance. We may perceive it as a very beautiful animal, or we may perceive it as an animal to be feared. What is it that determines whether we respond with fear? When we see a tiger, our memories of what we have heard about tigers and how dangerous they can be are activated together with the emotions with which we responded to that information. At the moment of seeing the tiger, our imprinted memories concerning tigers in our base consciousness are activated in a nonspecific way. This is part of why it is so difficult to notice the arising of fear at that moment. It is not our eyes, and it is not the object of the eyes that gives rise to the actual sense of perception. The eyes, the object, and our mind consciousness together form the sense perception.

When we have powerful memories associated with an object that we see, these memories will be activated and will dominate our mind consciousness. All the mind consciousness can contribute at that moment is the information that has been collected, reactivated, and merged with the present object of perception. This creates a sense of fear about the object. In the example of seeing a tiger, if we do not have any fearful memories when we see him, our perception will arise from our eyes, the tiger as the object of our eyes, and a mind consciousness that is clear and free of memories and preoccupations. The perception that arises then will be different. It may be free of fear. This does not mean that you walk up to the tiger to give him a hug or a pat. In fact, we need to be free from fear to be able to respond skillfully to a situation that threatens us. If we are overwhelmed by fear, our wisdom and clarity of mind will be obscured and we may become a victim of the threat.

We have collected many wholesome and unwholesome memories since childhood, birth, or even earlier. Some memories relate to experiences that have helped us develop wisdom of understanding, while others affect us and cause trauma. If we stay in touch with wholesome memories or qualities, this can help us make our life more meaningful and reduce our suffering. If we stay in touch with memories that are painful, this takes away our strength and makes us feel insecure and weak. Weakness can take different forms such as anger, depression, or anxiety, depending on the nature of the memory.

We do not want to be attached to past traumatic incidents, and we want to be free from suffering, yet sometimes we feel helpless in dealing with traumatic memories. What makes these memories active, strong, and fearful? We often remember situations from our early childhood. These situations no longer exist, yet the memories stay within us. We keep them alive by activating them over and over again. We may hold on to a particular memory and continue holding on, making it stronger in the process. In the case of a traumatic memory, we hold on to it because the situation was painful and we do not want to experience it again. We hold on to it because of our sub-conscious fear of getting hurt. We keep our memory alive and active to protect ourselves from getting hurt in a similar way, but we are not aware of the disturbing and exhausting effect of the memory we are keeping alive. Staying in touch with such memories means living with fear, and that is suffering.

If we wish to be free from the suffering caused by traumatic memories, we have to practice letting go. The practice of letting go can be done in many ways. It can be done through self-compassion or forgiveness. We may feel that the person or situation who hurt our feelings or threatened us and ultimately became the object of our fear may not deserve our forgiveness. However, we forgive so that we can be free from our suffering. There are so many people who have become the victims of fear or traumatic memories because they could not let go. They could not let go because they could not forgive.

Since we have elements in us that are responsible for the development of fear, we may feel that it will not be possible for us to be free from fear, but this is not the case. From the viewpoint of the Intimate Mind, fear is not separate from the true nature of our mind. It is a projection of our mind and does not exist independently. This makes it possible for us to let go of our fear and let it dissolve. Also, we can reduce the fear-related suffering in our life. We have a choice, and we have the potential to avoid making our life miserable through our addiction to fear. How can we do this? Most importantly, we must make up our mind to be more responsible for the happiness of our life and the peace of our mind. We have to empower this initiative thought so that we can free ourselves from the suffering we face.

SUBCONSCIOUS FEAR

Sometimes life is very demanding. The demanding nature of our work and responsibilities or of anything we are trying to accomplish can become the ground from which a sense of fear develops in us. This fear distances us from the initial motivation we may have had. We keep moving forward toward the accomplishment of our vision as though we were looking for the fruit but have forgotten to water the plant. We may be so carried away by our vision that we no longer pay attention to the people who work for us, including ourselves. Although this was not our intention, we become hard on ourselves and on others in the attempt to meet our needs. The intense demand we create through our fixation on our expectation obscures our innate compassion and our natural sense of caring for others and ourselves. Under this obscuration we become more and more vulnerable until we feel that every move others make affects us.

We need to remember that if we wish for fruit, we have to take care of the plant. When we take care of the plant, we will receive the fruit. The process of taking care of the plant is most important. If we do this with openness, love, and compassion instead of self-centeredness, there will be less distress in our life and in the lives of others.

Are you happy with what you are doing? Is it nourishing your life, your body, mind, and feelings? These are important questions to ask ourselves. As I walk into my home, am I the same person I was at work? Sometimes feelings of fear related to our work can be so subtle that we are not aware of them. We may even claim we are not experiencing any fear. On the other hand, our fear can also be so alive that we notice it easily.

Much of the time, our work may not be very demanding or exhausting, but by the end of the day, we feel torn apart. Is it the actual demand of our work that is exhausting us, or is there something else that needs to be brought into our awareness? Can we imagine how many different emotional states we go through during one single day of our work? If we could see our face each moment of the day, we might be surprised to see a multitude of emotional reactions that pass unnoticed by us. Every emotional reaction, although it may appear subtle, imprints itself into our consciousness. Even if an emotional reaction is very subtle, if we are constantly exposed to it, it disturbs our emotional stability. Emotional instability blocks the natural flow of energy in our body and mind. This puts pressure on the nervous system and on the functioning of the body. As a result we experience mental and physical exhaustion.

As for the nature of the mind, nothing can disturb it. It is the thinking mind that gets disturbed when we are under the influence of fear. Our thinking mind is the mind that feeds our judgment. Stress arises when our mind is fueled by subconscious fear. We may think that our feelings of stress are caused by the demands of our work, by our boss, workmates, employees, clients, the general work environment, or by the speed with which we have to carry out our work, but that is not actually the case. How is the feeling of stress created? Stress is a result of subconscious fear, the fear of not being appreciated or not being able to complete a task on time.

Feelings of stress arise from our addiction to fear based on self-judgment. We feel stress when our mind is divided. Simply carrying out an activity does not cause stress by itself. Feelings of stress arise when our mind is divided between an activity and expectation or judgment of our capacity. We constantly judge ourselves, and in this process of self-judgment we feed the conditioning that strengthens our fear. Feeling fear will not help us take care of the constraints imposed on us by the circumstances of our life. Our fear binds us with self-centeredness and does not allow us to receive each moment, each experience, and each person as they are. The nature of self-centeredness is criticism, judgment, and a lack of openness and love. Our resistance puts us into a state of mental and physical exhaustion. In the long run, this leads toward the suffering of depression and anxiety.

How can we reduce the fear and stress we experience when we have to fulfill certain tasks at our work, often with very little time? For example, as we do research, we may have to read through a large number of pages in search of specific information. While we do this, our habitual conditioning of judgment and expectation gives rise to attachment to finding the information we are looking for. Our grasping to the information we need and to our ideas of success and failure become stronger as we continue our search. Instead of being open to what is and relaxing into the moment, we let our mind be dominated by the desire to finish and to leave the task at hand behind. We may have to fulfill our task by a certain time. This does not mean that we cannot relax and that we cannot be free from fear. As for the Intimate Mind, we can be relaxed and at peace. This is part of our natural potential. Sometimes, our fear of not being able to meet the constraints of our situation takes away our confidence and our calmness. When our mind is calm and we abide in peace, our energy is more focused and clear. This will give us confidence to accomplish what we need to do, and to let go if we are not able to do something. If it is not possible for us to fulfill a given task, we have to accept this.

We may believe that only when we have completed the task at hand, we will be able to relax into the moment again. Our belief that we can relax only when something is accomplished can become the cause for a divided state of mind. When the mind is divided, we feel stress or fear. By the time we have completed the task we are exhausted. If we are unable to relax while carrying out our work, we can at least learn to become one with the joy and happiness of finally completing it. Then we can release all the tension, stress, and subtle emotional reactions that have built up during the process of our work. It is important to release the tension and feelings of stress that have built up in us during the day. Otherwise, our tension may give rise to different forms of suffering.

For example, we may be making a chocolate cake for the first time in our life. This may be difficult, especially if we worry whether our friend is going to like the cake. But in the end, when we present the cake to our friend, if she likes it, this can make us so happy that all our stress and fatigue dissolve in that very moment. Our joy may give us so much strength that we are able to bake another cake right away. If our friend does not like the cake, we may judge and hurt ourselves on top of the stress we have experienced while baking the cake. This is why we have to be strong, and why we have to release our mind from the grasp of expectation.

In order to become one with joy and be able to release our feelings of stress, we need to be aware of our emotional reactions, our tension, and the pressure we have put on ourselves. In the absence of self-awareness, these emotional states may remain so alive in us that they cause separation from our natural calm and peaceful state, even after the completion of the activity that caused us to feel pressured. For example, even when we are away from the workplace and trying to relax or sleep, the feeling of stress may still be subtly active in our body and nervous system, and this makes us unable to sleep or causes us to lose our appetite. We are under stress because we are constantly worried.

According to the Bön approach to healing, worry disturbs the proper functioning of the spleen. When the spleen is disturbed, this affects our stomach and pancreas. The spleen is connected to the earth element. Earth is stability. When we feel stressed and our spleen is disturbed, our earth element becomes imbalanced and we feel less grounded and insecure. Stress is one cause of imbalance in our earth element, and this imbalance causes the wind or air element in us to be overly active. When the earth and the wind or air element are in balance, we have stability.

To begin working with our emotional reactions and our fear, we need to keep our mind as stable and calm as possible. When the mind is in a state of calmness, it is free from fear at that particular moment. When there is calmness together with self-awareness, this puts an end to our fear. Self-awareness points out what causes us stress so that we know what is making us unable to relax. Self-awareness also means that we accept our state of being with compassion and self-care. Through self-awareness we will know what will help us and what is causing us to suffer. Once we know, we can work toward transformation.

We need awareness in order to not become a victim of our habitual conditioning of self-centeredness or insecurity that arises from our fear. Awareness is free of both aversion and holding on. Awareness brings everything into the field of clarity, so that we can see what disturbances are giving rise to fear in our life, or causing us to become the object of fear in the lives of others. This enables us to act more skillfully. Awareness is like a light that makes everything around it clearly visible. When we become one with awareness, our emotions and our state of mind are brought into the light, and we become familiar with what fear actually is, along with its causes. The true gift of awareness is that it allows us to abide in the realization of Open Presence, and to live with an undisturbed mind. When the mind is free from disturbance, there is no doubt, no grasping, and no fear.

Engaging in the act of mindfulness and keeping our mind open, flexible, and less judgmental of ourselves and others, are simple steps through which we can stay in touch with our innate awareness. To do this, we do not have to be perfect. All we need is to bring our mind and heart into what we are doing and into the situations we encounter. If a situation is demanding or gives rise to fear in us, we gently empower our awareness to connect with our innermost wisdom to stay calm and stable so that we can live and accept the moment as it is.

FEAR OF CHANGE

When we are afraid of something, we may think our fear is directed toward something external to ourselves, but often our fear comes out of a projection or a judgment. These projections and judgments are due to our deep-seated insecurity of self-judgment. Many different things characterize our insecurity. It can be our relationship with change, with sickness, with death, with separation from our loved ones, with uncertainty, or with failure to fulfill our dreams. Change can be fearful to live with. It is very important for us to become more familiar with the nature of impermanence in our life with the understanding of the Intimate Mind instead of resisting the changes we face. If we can do this, we can reduce the demanding and exhausting fear that arises out of thoughts related to change. With this understanding, we can bring more ease and joy into our life.

If there were no change, there would be no evolution. If there were no evolution, neither you nor I would exist. Since we exist within the continuum of change, what matters is how we can co-exist with the nature of change, so that change doesn't become the object of our fear. Change can allow us to see and understand the true nature of things and help us to wake up to the nature of existence.

How can change help us understand the true nature of reality? When we experience change in our life, this can either be associated with a positive or neutral perception that does not disturb our being, or it can stimulate an afflictive emotion such as fear, anger, or shock. For example, we may notice some new wrinkles as we look into the mirror in the morning. We might respond with judgment or fear. We might think that others may see us as less lovable because of our wrinkles. This is judgment, a story that we tie with the wrinkles. Our story makes our wrinkles an object of our fear. There will always be people who will love us in spite of our wrinkles, and ultimately, our wrinkles do not define who we are as human beings. Our perception of our wrinkles may also be neutral. We may recognize our wrinkles as part of the natural process of aging. If we do this, we perceive the nature of reality.

Since birth we have gone through so many changes. Some of these changes have given us joy and some fear. We constantly witness many changes that are happening around us, which may or may not have an effect on our individual lives. There are certain fears that are directly related to change, but our denial or inability to look into the nature of such fears makes them stronger and ourselves weak. When we fear the notion of change, we hide forever.

For instance, we may be in high school about to move on to college. We will face a big change. For some of us, it will be exciting and fun. Others may invite fear into our life and make ourselves miserable. When we look at the fear of change from this perspective, it is individually oriented. Fear of change is not universal but limited to the individual. This insight further allows us to understand that fear is not separate from the nature of our mind. We, in fact, have the potential by nature to understand it, work with it, and reduce the unnecessary pain and suffering. What separates fear from the nature of our mind? In the example of our fear of leaving high school, the fear may arise from our desire-attachment to our current situation, our addiction to habit, or our delusion. This delusion can be self-judgment or projected judgment of any kind.

Another aspect of fear of change concerns the process of aging and our attitude toward it. Many of us are not very comfortable with the truth of aging. Aging also reflects the nature of change. Our physical form, skin color, strength, sense power, strength of mind, and the range of opportunities available to us all go through changes within the continuum of aging. This is the very gift of life. Elderly people could be wiser because of their life experience. They could know better how to truly enjoy their lives. In the culture that I am from, we believe that when you grow older, you become a wisdom being. In the process of aging, we learn many things through our direct experience. The experiences we collect become our insight. We come to know that everything is impermanent.

In the natural world, when a plant reaches the stage of maturity, it blossoms and gives fruit, or it offers us shelter. When we are older, we have many things to offer to the world. Yet, we are not ready to accept getting older. We are caught up in the concept that we should look young, beautiful, and strong. We constantly force ourselves to fight against our own fate. Why do we struggle with ourselves and against the way of nature? What is pressuring us to think in this way? Is it really necessary?

So many questions arise in our mind regarding the changes we experience in our life. Sometimes we don't have an answer for all these questions, and so we wonder. The very act of wondering gives rise to fear and we begin to look for the answer all over again. We spend hours in front of the mirror to make ourselves look good with the deep hope that someone will like us. We dye our gray hair. We go to the gym. We wear different kinds of make up to cover our wrinkles, or we go through plastic surgery. Are these truly the answers we are looking for? Yes, we succeeded in making changes in our appearance, but did we succeed in making changes in our mind? Sometimes we make all kinds of changes in search of peace and happiness. Unfortunately, these very changes turn out to be a cause for more dissatisfaction and suffering, and inevitably push us into wanting further changes.

Why is it important to accept things the way they are, to accept change? In the above example, approaching our aging with acceptance is wisdom. This wisdom reduces our suffering. We accept the effects of the process of aging without being affected. The Buddha said to leave and accept things as they are. This also means to accept the way we are with care and compassion. Our care enables us to connect with ourselves. Our compassion helps us to recognize our suffering and the need for transformation. If we truly do this, we will find a way to put an end to our suffering.

FEAR AND NOT KNOWING

In addition to the changes we witness in our life, we are also afraid of changes that may or may not happen in the future. Fear of uncertainty and the unknown can be manipulative and exhausting because it is not based on our direct experience but limited to the thinking process in our mind. Our experience of fear may seem very real, but it is not based on an actual experience of the situation to which our fear refers. It is limited to the self and based on self-created assumptions or judgment. It is something we have created, and it has an effect on our life. We feel it because we put ourselves in that place, and we think that things are going to happen exactly the way we imagine.

For instance, we may want to be in a good relationship. Yet, we constantly judge ourselves, and consciously or unconsciously expect that the person we love will judge us in the same way. This is a self-created judgment that manipulates our life and takes away our strength to move into a relationship. When we fall in love, we no longer remain the person that we used to be. We become the manifestation of the feeling of love and its energy. For this to happen we have to be honest with ourselves so we can recognize our true feelings. Also, we have to be willing to let go of our past. Instead of clinging to past negative experiences and projecting them into the present, we can allow the love we feel in that moment to become the initiative strength of the journey that we are beginning.

In Zen Buddhism there is a saying that the mind of not knowing is a beginner's mind. Having a beginner's mind means approaching each moment and each thing without preoccupation by a view, concept, idea, or expectation. This is a very powerful practice. It puts an end to habitual conditioning which forces us to think and make the preconceived situation real in our mind, causing unnecessary pain and suffering in our life. Why is it that our views, concepts, and imagination become part of our delusion of ignorance, rather than a means of self-transformation toward the path of realization? It is because our conditioning in the form of desire-attachment to certain ideas causes our views to become obstacles or obscurations in the way of realization. Desire-attachment affects our mind and body and narrows down the path of possibilities we might consider otherwise. It does this by creating a wall of subtle aversion to anything that does not belong within the grasp of our personal desire realm. When we try to do or think about anything beyond this realm, we feel hesitation, insecurity, and lack of confidence. Together, these feelings manifest in the form of fear.

Beginner's mind does not mean forgetting the past. It means we do not allow the past to interrupt our experience of the present moment. The moment we start comparing the present with other moments in the past, we instantly create likes and dislikes. We create duality that, in turn, perturbs the purity of our experience. It is not our knowledge that narrows the available possibilities. It is our attachment to views, concepts, or a particular taste that exhausts the possibilities. Our attachment to the taste of chocolate ice cream may not allow us to appreciate other flavors.

SELF-CONFIDENCE AND FEARLESSNESS

The fear of uncertainty appears to be directed toward something outside of us, but this is not the case. Due to our internal insecurity, we habitually activate self-judgment. This further stimulates our insecurity and our fear of uncertainty. We think that fear of uncertainty comes from outside ourselves, but in fact, it arises because of our internal insecurity. What can we do to transform this habit of reacting and the fear that arises from it? When we have self-confidence, our mind doesn't easily get carried away or distracted by our habit of judgment and by our delusion.

We have to be true to ourselves. We have to know ourselves. We cannot know ourselves under the influence of insecurity and fear. To know ourselves we need to attend to our insecurity or weakness with love and compassion, and not turn away from or judge ourselves for it. Can we cultivate a quality of heart and mind that allows us to stay with a distressing situation and accept the discomfort that it causes us due to our insecurity? Can we stay with things as they are, without running away? When we are running away, we give power to the object from which we are running and to our own judgment; we reinforce our insecurity. This is like trying to run away from our own shadow on an open field.

As human beings we have a tendency to judge ourselves and to project onto others whom we admire or see as superior. We tend to want others to give us appreciation and acceptance in order to feel more secure, but actually, our insecurity is due to our own judgments of others as superior, and of ourselves as lacking in some way. If we can have more acceptance of ourselves just as we are, we won't feed our judgment, but rather will empower our inner strength. We will feel more relaxed, confident, and stronger, and the insecurity will dissolve.

We have to know our own gifts, our strength, our abilities,

and our innate wisdom. We must do this with compassion; otherwise it will become ego or pride. Once we really understand our qualities, our confidence will always be there for us, whenever we need it. That is self-confidence. Self-confidence is an inherent potential quality of the individual. It provides the strength and understanding we need when we are about to enter into the world of self-judgment and of judging others.

In developing our confidence it is important to live with the moment with honesty and dignity. Otherwise our experiences of the past or anticipations of the future will obscure our innate self-confidence and prevent our mind from being stable. When we are stuck in the past, this does not allow us to have self-confidence. Just because something happened in the past does not mean it will happen now—the future and the past are two different things. When we are afraid of something that has happened or we think will happen, our thinking about it actually forces us to experience our fear more strongly. We stop there. We never give ourselves a chance to get connected with the courage to go beyond this internal process. Rather, we repeat the cycle over and over again. In this way, we make our habit more rigid. We never have the confidence to engage in the actual act of manifestation. What would happen if we were to come out of the comfort realm of familiarity, out of our self-created world, and engage in the actual action and experience it for real? We would surely be able to make a better choice based on our direct experience. Then, if we really feel fear based on our direct experience of the situation, it is probably wise to pay attention to that. This is because here we are looking at the fear from a different, much more stable state of mind. In this case, we may be using fear as a measure of caution or self-security in the form of realizing the truth. This can protect us from becoming victims of unnecessary misfortune.

In the previous example of being afraid to leave high school, if we think back to when we first came to this school, we may recall that we hardly knew anybody. What happened was that we slowly, slowly made friends, and it became the best place on earth. Now we don't want to leave. To help us with any other situation, we can think about the change that we are about to face in the same way. Maybe there is so much waiting for you where you are going.

This is also similar to what happens when we meet people, but place unnecessary judgment onto them and distance ourselves from them. We never give ourselves a chance to know them. When we do, we do it with lots of expectations based on our own needs and our self-defined view of how things should be. Two different persons can't be one. They are two different individuals. Yet, the beauty of the human heart and mind is that we can learn to appreciate each other and to co-exist along with our differences. This is possible if we have faith and confidence in our strength, and if we do this with honesty, dignity, and respect.

FEAR OF DEATH

How many of us are afraid of being born? Isn't our birth something that we are happy about, a natural process and a gift of our human nature? At the same time, how many of us feel that death is not a natural process, and not a gift of our human nature? These questions make me wonder what difference it would make if we could accept death as an integral part of our human life.

Birth has its own natural potential to be harmonious, gentle, and natural. In the same way, death and dying have their own gifts and the potential to complete themselves in a very natural way. Our addiction to the fear of death doesn't allow us to see dying as a natural process and the reality of evolution. We make the process of dying very complicated, disturbing, and unnatural. In fact, this could happen with the process of birth, too. We could make the process of birth very difficult and unnatural by letting the fear of pain, uncertainty, and not knowing dominate the whole of our being. Under the control of fear, our natural strength of body and mind is dispersed. As a result, we become weak.

It is very important to live our lives fully while we can. We do not have to live with the fear of death. Do I know what will happen when I die? I really don't. Do I have to know it? No, I don't have to. This does not mean that there is no death. We all know that one day we will die, so why live in denial? We might use denial as an antidote and try to protect ourselves from our fear of death. But what about the denial itself? Denial is a subtle act of fear, and it is suffering. We cover the fear of death with denial, and then we have to find something else to cover our denial. This can go on forever. Meanwhile, we fall back into the cyclic continuum of suffering. We chase ourselves, while at the same time we run away from ourselves. It is important to stay in touch with the truth that one day we will die. We should not do this in such a way that it becomes the object of our fear, but so that it inspires us to appreciate our life and to live fully.

To enable us to be in touch with our mortality without making it an object of our fear, we need to familiarize ourselves more closely with what happens as we die. Once we are facing death this familiarity will help us to die without fear. In the Bön Buddhist tradition, we have 84,000 doors to liberation. The great number of different doors to liberation reflects the differences in our individual capacity and situation, in the phases of life we are going through, and the problems we are facing.

The common ground of these 84,000 ways of liberation is that they show us how to take care of ourselves and how to reduce the intensity of suffering and pain that is caused by the presence in us of afflictions such as ignorance, desire-attachment, hatred, jealousy, or envy. The teachings on the 84,000 doors to liberation explain how we can connect with our own potential of love, compassion, and a clear and calm heart and mind. These are the basic teachings that help us to free ourselves from the causality of suffering. They help us to prepare ourselves so that we are ready for the particular moment which is the moment of death.

The nature of death and the mystery of our previous lives have brought up many notions and feelings in us, and they can stimulate our emotions to a great extent. Since we do not know answers to the questions we may have about these things, they can stay with us as a source of fear. We fear that we do not have the necessary skill and wisdom to deal with our death. We make our death into an object of our fear, because we want to know about it with certainty. Sometimes dying can be painful and horrifying, but this does not mean that every dying process will be of this nature. We have to be strong and stable so that the fear of death does not take away our peace of mind and the strength of our life. According to the traditional Bön teachings on death and dying, "The Way of the Bön of Existence," there are 81 modes of death. Out of these 81, only one occurs with a natural cause. This is because we ourselves create the different kinds of afflictive conditioning that determine the causes of our mortality and the causes of future existences. Death due to a natural cause occurs when a person dies simply of old age.

On the one hand, we are gifted with our vital life force energy and the forces of the five elements in us. These constantly help and protect us from forces that would interrupt our life force energy. On the other hand, under the influence of ignorance and our egotistic self-centeredness we create an inner demon of fear. As a human being, each individual has three basic inherent elements: Mind or perceptual consciousness, potential life force energy of longevity, and vital essence of healing. When these elements are balanced in us, we enjoy a healthy life. It is essential to keep these elements pure and undisturbed. Instability of mind, lack of awareness, and the resulting strong feelings of desire-attachment or aversion constantly afflict us. Besides affecting our mind, they also put our life in constant danger of attack by the infinite provocation of energy. The provocation of energy is our process of working against the natural functioning of our own energy and the natural world around us. We do this by taking intoxicants, trying to control our feelings, and allowing afflictive emotions to take us away from our true nature. This can lead to disease or illness.

Any practice we do is at its heart focused on how to prepare ourselves for that particular moment of death. This is because we do not know when we will die. It is essential to keep that in our mind, and to be prepared for that moment of death. To do this, the first thing we need to do is overcome our fear of death. In order to overcome our fear we have to become familiar with death. We have to have more openness toward death, and we have to accept our own mortality. This acceptance has to take place not just in our mind. We have to accept the reality of our mortality with our heart and mind together and stay with that. Then the reality of our death does not alter our mind. Sometimes we say, "Oh, I accept death, and it does not cause me any fear." But in reality, how do we feel? Can we really let go of our denial and our fear?

Preparing ourselves for the moment of our death means that we have to prepare ourselves for each moment of our life. We don't know when the moment of our death will occur, so the continuum of our practice throughout every breath of our life is important. We have to become familiar with the situations that give rise to the notion of fear of death, such as the Four Great Uncertainties. The Four Great Uncertainties concern the place where we will die, the conditions of our death, the causes of our death, and the time when our death will occur. The pressure of the Four Great Uncertainties may feed our fear of death. Regardless of which phase of life we are in—infant, child, youth, or old age—we can suffer the pain of catastrophes such as murder, war, illness, epidemics, or accidents at any moment.

If we do not face and deeply accept the fact that we will all die, and that this could happen any time, we will feel afflicted and tormented. Our fear of death will take away our peace of mind and well-being. This will hinder our capacity to practice deeply and our capacity to invoke and connect with our life force energy and with the vital essence of healing. Therefore, it is very important that we become familiar with our mortality. Can we have the heart and mind to view our death in the same way we view our birth, as part of existence and as a natural process?

What does it mean to make ourselves familiar with the nature of death and the truth of our mortality? If we have made ourselves fully familiar with our death, the moment of our death will be what we call conscious dying. Conscious dying means dying with full awareness. Full awareness means having clarity of mind and freedom from the grasp of delusion, attachment, and other afflicted emotions. We are not attached to our family, friends, or the material belongings we leave behind in such a way that our attachment becomes an obstacle to the natural process of dying. Not being attached to our loved ones does not mean we do not care. Attachment is neither love nor care. Rather, can we have clarity of mind that allows us to appreciate the gifts of love and support that our friends, family, and material belongings have given us during our life? At the moment of death, can we take their presence as a strength to support us in meeting our death with peace?

It is extremely important at the time of death to have cleared any feelings of anger, hatred, or guilt we may have struggled with in our life. Conscious dying also means that we are free from fear, so that we can be with the moment completely and fully with our own freedom. Becoming one with the moment of death means that we are supporting this moment so that it unfolds in a natural way. Death is a natural process, and it has its own natural way of reaching completion. Our act of resistance or aversion in the form of fear or attachment to our life, family, and friends makes the process difficult. It is like putting up a wall to hold up the flow of a river.

To prepare ourselves for the moment of death, we can familiarize ourselves with the individual steps of the process of dying. In the Bön view of death, the death process begins with the dissolution of the elements into their sources. At this time, we may experience internal and external signs along with the three great visions of sound, light, and light rays.

First, the earth element begins to dissolve. When the earth element rolls back to its source, the spleen, which is associated with the earth element, ceases to function. When this happens, our body consciousness begins to withdraw. We feel heavy and can no longer raise our left arm. We may feel as though a mountain were pressuring us and may ask to have our pillow raised higher. At the same time, the energy center at our navel dissolves, and we may experience the appearance of yellow lights flashing and our surroundings moving. We lose control over our lips, and are no longer able to speak clearly.

This is followed by the dissolution of the water element. When the water element dissolves into water, the kidneys lose their function. We lose control over the nine orifices, we lose our sense of hearing, and we cannot raise our left leg anymore. At the same time, our genital energy center dissolves, and we lose control of the urinary function. The moisture of our body dries up and we can no longer hear. We may see blue lights flashing and hear different sounds.

After the dissolution of the water element, the fire element begins to dissolve.

When the fire element rolls back into fire, our liver stops functioning. We cannot raise our right arm any more. Our tongue becomes dry, and we lose our sense of taste and the sensation of our body heat. At the same time, the energy center at our throat dissolves, and we feel cold and experience a numbing sensation in our tongue. Blood may come out of our nose.

After the fire element has dissolved, the air element dissolves. When the air element rolls back into its source, our lungs lose their function. We lose our sense of smell, and we cannot raise our right leg anymore. At the same time, the energy center at the crown of our head dissolves, and we may see flashing green lights. At this point, the elements of time and space roll back to their origin, and our heart stops functioning. We lose our sense of sight and the energy of our brain. All the blood in the body rolls back to the heart. Then we exhale three times, darkness appears, and our head drops. This is the sign that the external death has finally come. Internally, our energy system is still intact. It takes a longer time for our energy system to dissolve.

At this point, the deceased person's consciousness enters into the Bardo of the fundamental base. Bardo is an intermediate state, such as the state between death and rebirth or between falling asleep and beginning to dream. According to the Bön tradition, there are different kinds of Bardo states. In this Bardo there is only darkness. It is similar to falling asleep. The first stage of our sleep is strong and deep. Later, vision slowly begins to arise, just as in our sleep dreams begin to arise.

During the process of the dissolution of the elements, if there is somebody present who can read out the Bardo Thodrol, the teaching on liberation through hearing, this will be of great help to the dying person. Even when our physical sense of hearing has departed, our consciousness that is transmigrating from death to birth is able to hear this teaching. The Bardo Thodrol is the instruction to the dying person not to fear and not to get distracted as the elements continue to dissolve. It is the instruction to remind the dying person to recognize that whatever he or she hears, sees, or experiences is the true manifestation of his or her own awareness. So there is nothing to fear. This is followed by the practice of Phowa, which is the transference of our consciousness.

At the time when we die, this is the only true moment. There is nothing beyond that moment. Thinking about something else would be distraction and will create obstacles that block the natural process of dying. Our practice is to accept this very moment. Both the person who is dying and others who are supporting the dying process need to accept this moment as it is. There is a profound practice of being with others who are dying. In this practice we take care of the dying person with love and compassion. We might not be able to stop the person from dying, but we help the dying person to meet her or his death peacefully, and we help to make the process less fearful and easier. By being the strength and confidence of the dying person, we can make the process gentle and natural. Beyond that, if we are with a dying friend with an open, unafraid mind, this will help us to look at our own mortality with less fear.

CHAPTER 7

MAKING CLEAR DECISIONS

Dispelling the darkness of confusion
by making clear decisions
is the strength of the Intimate Mind
that brings us back to our innate perfection.

REMAINING IN THE STATE OF CLARITY
WITH CONFIDENCE

Once there was a little princess who lived with her two older sisters and her parents, the king and queen, in a beautiful palace. When the three princesses grew into young women, everybody said that they were very beautiful. But the youngest was the loveliest of them. The two older ones soon had many admirers and the king and queen selected suitable husbands for them. Then only the youngest and most beautiful daughter was left. She was indeed so beautiful that the king was concerned that if he married her to one of her many wealthy and powerful admirers, the others might wage a war on him out of jealousy. He consulted with his ministers about what he should do, and it was decided that they would cast lots so that every man in the country would have a chance to have the princess as a bride.

When the morning of the great day had come, the princess went into the palace garden all by herself. As she stopped by a little pond, suddenly a beautiful bird shining in all the colors of a rainbow landed next to her.

The bird began to speak and said to her, "Little princess, I want to tell you a very precious secret. Today is the day when your husband will be chosen for you. My advice to you is to make up your mind that you will remain faithful to your parents' decision and stay with the husband that will be chosen tonight and never deviate from that decision."

The little princess listened very carefully to what the bird was telling her and thanked the bird. Then the bird disappeared, and the princess went back into the palace to braid her hair and put on her most beautiful dress.

When the time to cast lots had come, the big palace hall was filled with men of all ages and from all sorts of different backgrounds. They were all putting their names on pieces of paper and into a big urn. Even the poor beggar Shik Tsang, filthy, foulsmelling and covered with lice, was there to try his luck. Finally the king picked the name of the husband-to-be from the urn and read it out. It was Shik Tsang. Everybody was dismayed and didn't feel like celebrating. So the little princess took a few of her belongings and set off with Shik Tsang.

Shik Tsang took her all the way through the big forest surrounding the palace grounds. They had to walk on foot, as Shik Tsang did not own any horses or carriages. The princess was not used to walking this much and soon became very tired, but she went along quietly and cheerfully. Then they crossed a vast plain, and finally reached another forest. When they were well into the forest, they finally came upon a tiny run-down hut with a broken roof.

"This is where I live," said Shik Tsang.

There was no door so they just walked in and the princess saw immediately that the whole place was covered with filth and mud, and there was a strong stench in the air. She had to pull up her dress to protect it from touching the mud, but even so she couldn't quite prevent the hem from getting dirty.

Shik Tsang pointed to a half-broken ladder that led upstairs, and she followed him into a small chamber upstairs. "This is our bedroom," he said.

Instead of a bed there was some dirty, old straw on the floor, and the smell was almost as bad as downstairs. Shik Tsang gestured for the little princess to sit down on the straw and then asked her, "Dear, how do you like your new home? I hope it is not too simple for you?"

The princess replied, "It is fine. I am with you, and the rest really does not matter so much."

"Are you sure?" he asked.

"Yes, I am sure about this," the little princess responded.

When she had answered in that way, Shik Tsang reached for her hand, and she let him take it. Then he said, "Now it is time for our wedding celebration. I want to ask you to close your eyes and not open them again until I tell you. Please do not open your eyes, even if you hear sounds that make you feel frightened."

So the princess closed her eyes firmly. Soon she heard a loud rumble, followed by loud thundering noises. The sounds became louder and louder, until she thought that for sure the old hut would now collapse and bury them under falling trees and rocks. But she held to her promise and kept her eyes closed.

Finally she heard Shik Tsang say, "Now, my love, you can open your eyes again."

The princess opened her eyes and gasped in wonder. She was no longer in the old hut, but instead in a huge, magnificent palace—even more stunning than the palace in which she had lived with her parents. All the filth was gone, and instead there were soft carpets, silken canopies, and exquisite furniture. The air was filled with the fragrance of sandalwood, and she could hear birds chirping outside in the palace gardens. Then she turned to look at Shik Tsang. To her great surprise, Shik Tsang was no longer dirty and clad in rags, but had transformed into a very handsome young prince dressed in silk and velvet.

The prince took her hand and said, "Dear, because you have been so patient you shall now be rewarded with a splendid wedding celebration." So they went together into the big palace hall where a great feast awaited them.

How could the princess who had grown up surrounded by all sorts of comforts and riches be able to accept a filthy beggar as her husband, and a dirty, smelly hut as her home? No doubt she had grown up expecting she would marry a prince or someone very rich and beautiful. How could she be that calm, steadfast, and accepting? This was possible because from the very start, from the moment when the bird talked to her, she completely cleared her mind and placed it firmly on the intention to stay with the husband that would be selected for her regardless of her own expectations.

Usually, when we make a decision, it is because we think it will create circumstances that will bring us happiness, or we envision a set of conditions we believe will bring us happiness and then try to bring about these conditions. Yet, any specific thing or condition can only give us limited happiness. We may find that we had the wrong idea about the condition we were trying to effect, and that it does not bring us the happiness we expected. Even if it does, the happiness will not last because the conditions of our happiness are impermanent. Eventually we are bound to meet with obstacles. If we made our decision because we thought it would lead to pleasant circumstances, we may at this point start to lose interest and no longer stick to our decision. We may begin to search for other possibilities and conditions that seem to promise more happiness. We start to doubt ourselves and lose our strength, and our decision falters.

The power of the princess in the above story came from her commitment to her decision, independent of what the outcome might be. This is an ability we can consciously strengthen in ourselves.

Many of us may have come to our practice, or to a spiritual path, because we are looking for a way to end the suffering in our life. It is wonderful if this motivation leads us to begin a path of spiritual practice, but this also has its limitations. When we follow a path of spiritual practice, we may face hardships. When this happens, we may judge ourselves and doubt our decision to follow a spiritual path. This questioning might distance us from our motivation. Our path of practice may also show us our own limitations that are due to our conditioning. Having to realize our limitations will cause us suffering. We must be very open and willing to change in order to overcome this conditioning.

Sometimes, out of our urge to be free from suffering, we hold on to a glimpse of our true nature and may reject the current state of our mind. Due to our conditioning we may not recognize that what we have glimpsed is actually our true nature that is always with us. It is also possible that we develop an attachment to the particular conditions that were present when we experienced such a glimpse. This is why in the Bön tantric practice we unify our experience of bliss with emptiness, so that we do not create a new conditioning based on the expectation that a particular situation will bring us in touch with our true nature. Since it is our true nature, it can be manifested anytime, anywhere, without relying on a particular condition. Yet, this is only possible if we recognize our true nature for what it is.

If we do not have this recognition, this means we do not really have confidence in our true potential, and we have not really understood that the state we are longing for or that we may have glimpsed is simply our true nature. Instead we have turned it into something separate from our mind of the here and now.

This is why a wholesome and clear motivation is important. If we feel motivated to practice in order to liberate ourselves and others from the suffering caused by the two delusions of ignorance and intellect, this motivation may be strong enough to allow us to clear our mind and heart. Then we are able to accept whatever the path brings us. This motivation is the understanding that helping others is no different from helping ourselves. Helping others and finding joy and happiness in that is a true act of a compassionate being that transforms our subconscious afflictive emotions. Truly helping ourselves, on the other hand, requires that we free ourselves from the grasp of the five afflictive emotions. Once we are free from afflictive emotions we do not have to do anything to help others. Our very act of freeing ourselves from delusion is itself profoundly helpful. Without this motivation it is possible that in the process of helping ourselves we might subconsciously strengthen our conditioning. In this case, we are neither helping ourselves nor others, but are creating a condition for suffering.

If our primary motivation is to learn to be more compassionate and recognize our true nature of selflessness, it becomes possible to learn from every experience in our lives. If our motivation is to overcome the delusion of self and other, then our mind can remain clear, strong, and stable, even as we encounter difficult circumstances. The Bön teachings tell us not to despair if we try to help others and our efforts do not work out. True compassionate beings never give up, even if their efforts to help someone are not successful for many lifetimes. This is because they have recognized the true nature of their mind and have decided to remain in that state with confidence and clarity.

TOUCHING OUR INNATE PERFECTION
THROUGH CLEARING OUR MIND

Our capacity to have a clear mind does not depend on our circumstances. If we try to do something and our mind is not clear, difficulties will make us feel torn between what we are trying to accomplish and our feelings of doubt, resistance, or exhaustion.

Once we become aware that these feelings arise because our mind is divided, we will be able to clear our mind. I feel lucky that I was sent to a monastery when I was a little boy, because every teaching I received there was about clearing my mind and about how to respond to difficult situations. Growing up in the monastery provided me with an education, taught me how to love and be loved, how to be compassionate, and how to accept things without fear. Life there was also difficult. There wasn't enough food, we had no warm clothes, living space was very limited, and the facilities were very simple and rudimentary. I lived with 50 other kids in one big dorm room. During the monsoon season the rain would drip through the roof, and we had to place pots everywhere to catch it. This would not solve the problem of the water coming through the chimney into the stove in the kitchen and killing the fire on which we were trying to cook! I remember vividly how we would take turns baking the bread for the whole community of 50 boy monks. It was very challenging, but it was also deeply inspiring. Sometimes we spent the whole night making bread.

Living in the monastery was an experience of continuous learning. I received a great gift from those moments in the kitchen. I understood that I could choose to be sad or to panic, but reacting like this would not solve the problem. To solve the problem I needed to look deep inside myself and make a clear decision with wisdom and self-compassion. I needed to refrain from making choices that would lead me into the emotional chaos of fear, despair, or self-judgment. Being patient instead gave me the strength and inspiration needed to bake 50 loaves of bread under almost impossible conditions. Making clear decisions informed by wisdom allowed me to have compassion toward myself and be able to say, "Tempa, it's okay"—whatever the situation. It is this process that gives me strength and allows fresh streams of insight to flow like dolphins swimming across the deep blue ocean. When we make clear decisions, the circumstance or situation itself becomes the inspiration for this process of developing the clear mind of wisdom; it becomes just like the water that allows the dolphin to swim freely and easily through it.

Through making clear decisions we can learn to work skillfully with whatever we are facing at that very moment, so that we can keep our minds clear and undisturbed. We can find the strength to live fully in this present moment. We can decrease the unnecessary distress that results from our projections about the future, and we can free ourselves from the pain and suffering that arise from attachment to past events. There are myriad small situations in our daily lives that pressure us in subtle ways. Often this occurs without our noticing it. The result is that our reactions are imprinted into our base consciousness in the form of karmic traces.

There may also be distinct and traumatic past experiences that we have not been able to let go of. When we face a situation that is beyond our ability to understand or accept, this can shock us and cause unbearable damage in our life. Often, we hold on to this experience of shock, and it becomes a permanent source of pain to us. Recovering from our trauma may take us years. It could even take us a lifetime. Keeping such trauma alive is one of the most painful things that can happen in an individual's life.

What happens inside us when something shocks us? At that very moment, our energy is dispersed in ten thousand directions. When the totality of the energy has dispersed, it destroys the innermost space that keeps our mind, heart, and body unified. When this occurs, we are torn apart. Our mind and heart move in a different direction than the body, and we may be affected in many ways.

This does not have to take place in the form of a big incident. Even a small reaction that happens in our everyday life can tear apart our heart and mind. The memory of a painful situation we have not been able to let go of can haunt our peace of mind, our trust, and our beliefs, and place us in a vulnerable state in which afflictive emotions can take advantage of our condition. Unresolved memories can take us far from our innate potential and our natural strength to trust and believe, to experience love and compassion, and to heal ourselves. Without our noticing it, we may be hiding from ourselves, from our friends, and from the world. Sometimes these memories imprison us and won't let us live or die with a clear mind.

If we know the practice of clearing our mind, we can ask ourselves if it is possible to liberate these haunting memories. I think this is something we all can do. If we are able to turn a small incident into a haunting memory, then surely there is also potential within us to resolve it. We need to recognize how the incident has gained so much power over us and why it continues to hold this power. We need to understand how it is affecting our life. We can make peace with a haunting memory by asking ourselves these questions. When we ask these questions, this implies the motivation to work toward transformation. We ask because we have accepted that there are difficulties in our life.

The next step is to become aware that we are not alone in our suffering, but that there are many beings on this planet who have been swept away by ripples of misfortune. Reaching this level of awareness can help us wake up from our suffering. This will not only help us find our true nature, but it will also help others who are still immersed in suffering. There is a space for change and choice, always. In The Buddha's teachings on the Four Noble Truths he stated that there is suffering. Where there is suffering, there is a cause of suffering. Where there is a cause of suffering, there is also a way of transformation. We ourselves are neither the haunting memory nor a ripple of misfortune. We become what we think and what we practice. If we are able to let go of the past and give space to the present moment, this can take us into a phase of a new beginning:

Miracles happen,
healing does happen
any time any moment,
within the spontaneity of continuum.

If we have been introduced to practices that help us let go of unhealthy or disturbing past experiences, it is important that we help those who are ignorant of such means and who are oppressed by fear. We also need to help ourselves. Our problems make us feel that we can only be far from perfect. Yet, we all are already perfect within, as we are all Buddha from the very beginning of evolution. It is this innate perfection that we can touch through the practice of clear decisions. In the deepest sense, through clearing our mind with respect to the situations we encounter in our daily lives, we free our mind from the obscuration of ignorance.

PART III

MANIFESTING THE INTIMATE MIND

I do not need to know
suffering or happiness.
I do not ask for a spiritual breakthrough
or extinction of cyclic existence.
All I asked for
is a glass of water
and you brought
the whole of the oceans
the sunshine
cloud rain
deep mountain forest.
Imagination of my fantasy
swims across the deep blue ocean.

CHAPTER 8

THE HIDDEN WISDOM

To be intimate with each thing
allows all beings
to touch their hidden wisdom
and realize their true nature.

We are all born with innate wisdom. Our wisdom is hidden in that it is an innate potential, but it does not automatically become manifest. A number of obstacles can prevent us from becoming aware of this innate potential and from developing it. We have given too much power to our insecurities, our fears, our lack of confidence, and our self-centeredness. Under the control of these emotions, we lose the space and the strength that are available within us to manifest our wisdom. Our wisdom is hidden, because our ignorance and the resulting afflictive emotions corrupt the true nature of our mind. Ignorance prevents access to our innate wisdom; it forces us to doubt its existence.

Some conditions are better hidden if we are not ready to take care of them. In the case of wisdom, however, the more it is exposed, the more it retains its quality of clarity. The more we use it, the sharper it becomes, and the more it falls into the place where it belongs.

PROVIDING SPACE FOR THE HIDDEN WISDOM

The Intimate Mind says:
You do not have to accept
and you do not have to reject either.
All I ask is for a little space
where I could come and go,
where I could fall and rise,
and where I could manifest and dissolve.

Flexibility of mind is a skillful means through which we can provide the space for our hidden wisdom and the wisdom of others to manifest. Sometimes we do not respect another's wisdom because of our jealousy, pride, or self-centeredness. If we can make space to perceive and respect another's wisdom from our heart, this will help us to transform our self-centeredness, and it will help the other person to feel confident in manifesting his or her wisdom.

When our mind acquires the quality of flexibility, it radiates acceptance and understanding and thus invites also the wisdom of others to manifest. This then opens the door to another space where our mind can begin to cultivate the quality of genuine tenderness and softness. This leads us into a deeper feeling of ease and allows us to relax into this very moment. Flexibility, acceptance, and tenderness free us from our addiction to seriousness. When our mind is flexible, it provides a space where all our sense fields can function, not interfering with each other, but rather, supporting each other in experiencing a quality of clear perception. Then, our experience will be the feeling of one taste*. This is the quality of mind I call openness. When the mind is open, we see the beauty of perfection in each other and in all things. At the same time, we also see suffering and its causes and conditions in our lives and in the lives of others with more clarity. Openness allows us to connect with everything. Feeling connected with others can take us to a state of mind where we experience the gift of our true nature in the form of eternal joy. This experience of joy allows us to access the part of ourselves that is a state of purity, free of judgment and criticism. This purity protects us from delusional attachment and aversion. When we are free of attachment and aversion, we recognize our oneness with everything.

Clarity, the unification of our innate purity and our eternal joy, is another distinct quality of our true nature. Clarity allows us to perceive that you and I are not separate. It allows us to distinguish between conditions that cause suffering, such as our afflictions, and those qualities that lead us toward transformation. Purity is a state of mind that is free from the two types of delusion. Clarity is the capacity of the mind to recognize and understand a pure state of mind in ourselves and others.

How can we experience clarity as our true nature? When we are free from the grasp of the two delusions, we experience clarity. When we are free from the grasp of the two delusions, we become Buddha. At that point, we know that clarity is our true nature. Clarity is always there, but in most of us it is covered by our obscurations. To uncover our true nature we need to become aware of how our obscurations arise, and we need to become familiar with what is causing them. We need to closely observe the mental, physical, and emotional components of our reactions every time we react

---

* One taste is the experience of the nondual mind that does not differentiate between objects according to subjective preferences or judgments.

or respond to a situation. If we combine clarity with compassion, we will be able to observe not only our own state of being, but also the state of other beings and how they are affected by our actions.

For example, the Mississippi and the Rio Grande are both rivers. They both have the nature of water and finally enter into the deep blue ocean. It is the path of their journey that makes them unique and different from each other. It is the process of their journey that provides for the beauty of their uniqueness. Entering into the great ocean, the individual identities of the Mississippi and Rio Grande dissolve, and they return back to their true nature of oneness. The compassion and kindness of the great ocean provides a space for these two unique rivers to unify into oneness. How can we manifest this process, how can you and I provide that space within ourselves that allows us to live in harmony with ourselves, with each other, and with all beings? How do we develop that space within that allows love and compassion to take root in us, so that dualistic reactions like trust and mistrust, ease and fear, acceptance and judgment, can withdraw their grasp from our mind and heart? How can we cultivate a space that allows heart and mind to become one? Our heart and mind alone, without the presence of the other, are each incomplete. Similarly, mind and body are interdependent. They both are needed to make our perceptions a palpable reality.

To be able to provide a space for others and also for our own feelings is such a beautiful practice. Can we become like the great ocean that welcomes and embraces all the unique rivers and all the beings that take refuge in it? Unlike the ocean, as human beings, sometimes we do not provide that space, but instead hold on to our identity and pride. This invites the cloud of misunderstanding and misperception between the world and ourselves that leads to a feeling of separation. I believe that we are not separate from each other but are one. At the same time, I understand that we are unique individuals. This is precisely the set of circumstances that provides the possibility of aspiring to and cultivating the compassionate heart:

> *I keep my heart and mind*
> *wide open*
> *to bear witness to the gift*
> *of your being,*
> *whatever form you manifest*
> *at that very moment.*

WISDOM AND CONDITIONING

Being human and being in this world is a gift. As human beings, we are gifted with wisdom as our inherent true self, and this self is not one, and not two. It is not something that we can grasp or hold on to. It is just the all-pervasive essence of being. By nature it is luminous, non-abiding, and all-pervasive within the continuum of time and space. It is simply the union of all our innate wholesome qualities that we inherited from the beginningless continuity of primordial existence. We are all born with this wisdom, and we are not separate from it. However, our existence is marked by impermanence; and thus it reflects the nature of change and evolution within the continuum of each individual life.

We are all part of this wisdom—but sometimes we mistake ourselves as the whole and then perceive ourselves as separate and lose sight of being part of that greater whole. This mistaken perception is caused by the emotional reactions we have to different events we encounter. Our attachment to these emotional reactions then obscures our awareness that we are not separate. Every change we experience affects our capacity to stay in touch with our wisdom. Our wisdom itself is without change, but our perception of it is affected by the changing flow of our emotions.

Unable to recognize the underlying truth of how changing conditions affect our relationship with our inherent wisdom, we lose the connection to our potential, and we wander into the chaos of external distractions and internal addictive fantasies. Sometimes though, while riding the waves of chaos, distraction, or addictive fantasy, we touch our innate wisdom, and this enables us to see how our afflictive emotions obstruct the openness of our heart and mind. Touching our innate wisdom gives us the strength to make clear decisions. It is like the sun that brings everything into the light and illuminates the all-pervasive awareness that is part of our true nature. When we pay attention to everything in the field of our awareness without the destructive judgment that separates self and other, the strength of our awareness itself increases. Self-awareness is the essence of our inner wisdom being. It makes it possible for us to know the source of eternal joy. Thus, it also illuminates the causes and conditions that give rise to suffering and pain.

Sometimes, we allow unnecessary suffering and pain into our lives, simply because we are not aware at the very moment of making a choice. This lack of awareness of our innate wisdom manifests itself in the form of ego and self-centeredness. Wisdom is necessary to recognize and manifest our selflessness. The wisdom of self-awareness is rooted in equanimity, whereas ego or self-centeredness is rooted in desire-attachment and limited view. When our view is limited, we narrow down the pathway of wisdom and close our heart. Sometimes we keep our heart closed because of our fear of getting hurt, and, keeping our heart closed, we suffocate in our closed heart and become prey to depressive loneliness.

On the basis of our projected judgment, we tend to grasp onto objects, and thus obscure the Intimate Mind, resulting in mental categories such as like and dislike or acceptance and rejection. We judge the perceived object to be good or bad, happy or sad, joyful or painful, and we feel love or hatred. Engaging in this dualistic way of perceiving, we develop the corresponding emotional behaviors which get imprinted into our base consciousness in the form of conditioning or as karmic traces. Through our overexposure to karmic traces in everyday life, these traces become habitual energy-patterns that obscure the Intimate Mind like clouds obscure the sun, so that we can no longer perceive its natural heat and light.

If we want to increase our awareness of our conditioning, it is fortunate if we have the opportunity to observe it in action. A friend of mine told me about a restaurant where the cook flips the omelet in front of the guests. Sometimes the omelet falls off the pan. Is this a reason to feel scared or embarrassed? To me, it is just an omelet that fell out of the pan. What is it that causes us to feel embarrassed or scared? Maybe it is our ego. Maybe it is our habitual addiction to the concept of perfection, or the pride of some self-defined idea of personal success. Maybe we are judging our capacity and feel that others will think we are not good enough. We may think that feeling embarrassed will help us not to drop the omelet again. Yet feeling embarrassed or scared is not a healthy way of protecting ourselves from unfortunate or unwholesome actions. It is best to have a positive way of transforming. Using a positive antidote is the Buddha Way.

Reactions of judgment, embarrassment, or feeling scared arise because of our conditioning. We need to notice how our conditioning affects our physical, mental, and emotional state at that very moment. We may feel scared and embarrassed. Yet, often, it does not end there. Rather, it becomes a mental preoccupation leading us into further distraction. And the omelet is flipped onto the floor once again. Moreover, the energetic influence of the incident stays with us for a longer period of time. We encounter so many situations of a similar nature in our everyday lives. To let these situations affect us is exhausting. Fortunately the precious gift of being human is that we can learn from our experiences; we have a choice to not let the situation and our response to it obscure the true nature of our mind.

The Buddha said, "All you have to do is to take care of your mind, and you will take care of this world." Since then, we have all tried, we still do, and we will continue to try. Hundreds and thousands of unique methods, techniques, and spiritual practices have been developed. Many different traditions and schools have emerged, just to take care of this mind. Do you think that by taking care of one's mind one can take care of the world? And if you knew that this is possible, how would you do it, where would you begin? Maybe your way of doing it would be different from mine. That is the beauty of being you and me. This recognition of our uniqueness provides the space for our wisdom of understanding.

THE INNATE WISDOM THAT CUTS THROUGH DELUSION

As compassionate beings, we have the potential to be free from the delusion of affliction. Compassion is one way to overcome the delusion of affliction. However, in the absence of wisdom, even if we are compassionate, generous, and stable, we can still be affected by the delusion of intellect, and thus our compassion remains limited. For instance, we may feel compassion only for our family and friends. If we have wisdom, our compassion is universal and no longer makes any distinction. At this point, our compassion is the natural expression of our recognition that we are all not separate. This is wisdom.

The delusion of intellect is our attachment to different kinds of views and judgments. It is like a dark cloud that hides the sun from our view. Wisdom, on the other hand, allows us to maintain clear vision and understand the true nature of both relative and absolute phenomena. In order to maintain awareness of our wisdom and in order to overcome the delusion of intellect, it is extremely important for us to not rely on our compassion alone but also the practice of skillful means: the unification of compassion and wisdom. If we neglect the practice of skillful means, we could be consumed by the delusion of intellect and become so attached to a specific method or result that our wisdom and our potential to be clear are completely obscured. We may start to operate without respecting what other people are saying and without considering whether our actions will really bring happiness to ourselves and others.

One of my best friends from childhood was a true compassionate being who very sincerely wanted to serve his village and his people with his whole capacity of loving kindness and deep understanding. One time while on a short vacation from the monastery I visited my village. I had the opportunity to meet and reunite with my friend. During our visit he explained to me that he believed that it is up to the people of the village to improve their village themselves. So he had started initiating this beautiful thought and he was trying to convince every person in the village. I was very touched and inspired by his motivation. A year later I heard that my friend had joined the Maoist rebels, thinking that in this way he could serve the village better, and that the Maoist movement would bring peace and prosperity into the lives of people. The Maoist manifesto emphasized economic equality for all, and that very idea had attracted him. Although his initial intention was to improve the conditions for his fellow villagers and he was guided by compassion, he eventually found himself on a path of violence, still believing that this would bring peace to his village.

This is an example of how we can become so attached to our ideas or expectations that we totally forget and disconnect from the initial motivation that gave birth to these expectations. In fact, in this case we are not only forgetting our motivation, we are also unable to recognize how our actions may actually bring forth the opposite effect of what we had intended. Once we have strayed this far from awareness, even when someone tries to point out the discrepancy between our original intention and the effect our action has in the context of the situation, we are not willing to listen to him or her. Rather we become defensive. In this way, if we are too attached to our view or expectation, things go wrong without our noticing. When we finally become aware that the situation did not work out the way we had expected, we refuse to accept our responsibility for this. Typically we are conditioned so that we don't know how to accept our mistakes; to become aware that we made a mistake makes us feel uncomfortable and insecure. If we do find the strength to accept our mistake and notice where we are, this will help us to move beyond the threshold of insecurity and fear with which we have been holding ourselves back.

Sometimes our superficial way of defining who we are can take us into an extreme. It is important to know who we really are. So what does this question of "who am I, really" mean to you? This is indeed a very complex question. As mentioned, things change continuously. Nothing really remains the same. When considering this question from this perspective, it would be difficult to find one label that defines who we are. Once upon a time, I was a little boy. Now I am in my thirties. But it is not only the age that changes. My physical, mental, and psychological states also change. They change, just like the leaves of a tree that passes through the seasons: from early spring, when the leaves are just emerging from their buds, to summer, when they are fully matured in their shape and depth of color. From summer they pass to autumn, when they prepare for the completion of the cycle. Finally, by winter, this simple process has reached completion. So then, who am I? What part of this journey is to be referred to as "I"? Should I label myself according to how I feel right now? Or according to what I have been doing so far in my life, or what I aspire to become? Or should I define myself according to my physical appearance, my gender, or according to the spiritual tradition that I follow?

If we define ourselves according to how we feel, or according to some personality characteristics that we see in ourselves, we easily end up becoming very self-critical. For instance, if I consider myself to be a shy person, I may believe that my difficulties are caused by my shyness, and I might blame myself for the difficulties that I am experiencing. This is not necessary. Instead, we can keep our heart and mind open and accept how we are without judgment. If we can do this, the duality between our present perception of ourselves and our perception of how we would like to be will dissolve. Then, we will be guided by wisdom. Sometimes, rigidly holding on to some constructed concept of self can lead to a strong attachment in us. But if we become aware of this attachment to such self-definition, we can realize selflessness.

Concepts do not reveal reality. We construct the concept of, for example "war" in order to bring peace, and the concept of "practice" to transform the suffering and pain in our lives. Concepts are thoughts mixed with ego. If any kind of thought mixes with our ego on the basis of self-centeredness, desire-attachment, or ill intention, it becomes delusion. Delusion keeps our innate wisdom hidden forever. Only if our concepts are based on awareness can they lead to non-conceptual awareness that has the power to directly experience reality. Non-conceptual awareness matches both the external reality and the internal perception of true experience.

There is no doubt that wholesome motivation can bring joy into our life and thus into the world. Yet, a wholesome motivation alone—without wisdom and compassion—can also lead to suffering. It is only when our actions are based on wisdom and compassion that we can overcome the dualistic perception of, for instance, joy and suffering, self and other, action and intention. Wisdom makes it possible for compassionate beings to recognize that we are all not separate. This recognition clears all notions of extremes, and thus it clears our attachment to specific means and methods and to specific definitions of ourselves.

This is particularly true of the wisdom called "discriminating wisdom." Discriminating wisdom is an antidote for desire-attachment, and it leads us toward self-transformation. By nature, discriminating wisdom is within each of us. Yet, it is as hidden to us as if it did not exist at all. Under the strong influence of desire-attachment, we succumb to our mental and emotional instabilities. We are distracted by the desired object or by our desire for a projected fantasy, without knowing and understanding the consequences. With the gift of discriminating wisdom, we can penetrate the shield of desire-attachment and enter into the deeper layer of reality.

In order to actualize this discriminating wisdom, we need the help of mirror-like wisdom and the wisdom of equality. Mirror-like wisdom is the ability to reflect each object exactly as it is without distortion and without becoming distorted oneself. Thus, the true nature of mirror-like wisdom is not affected by the multitude of objects it encounters. The wisdom of equality is our capacity to leave things as they are with equanimity. Discriminating wisdom is like the body of a bird, while the wisdom of equality and mirror-like wisdom are the bird's two wings. All three are needed for the bird to be able to fly. When these three are present together, discriminating wisdom allows us to investigate our every encounter with the stability provided by our mirror-like wisdom and with the equanimity provided by our wisdom of equality. When our mirror-like wisdom is stable enough to reflect objects without distortion and without becoming distorted, then discriminating wisdom allows us to investigate these objects and events skillfully and to our benefit. For example, we may be attracted to tantric practice of meditation, but our discriminating wisdom may tell us not to do the practice right away, but to try first to understand it thoroughly through skillful investigation. We carry out this investigation with the help of mirror-like wisdom. If we are not stable or secure, the intensive nature of the circumstances we encounter could distract, disturb, and affect us strongly.

How can we be like a mirror that remains unaffected by the intensity of what we encounter externally, and the insecurity, fear, lack of confidence, doubt, or past memories we encounter internally? Staying unaffected does not mean being unconscious. It does not imply an "I don't care attitude." Rather, we do our best not to let anything cause us suffering. We do our best not to let anger, hatred, jealousy, or any other disturbing emotion distort our perceptions and reactions. As human beings we have the potential to be with our wisdom, and equally, we have the potential to fall into our shadow and remain in a state of ignorance that causes us to be controlled by our afflictions. We do have a choice. And the choice that we make determines whether we will connect with our wisdom and overcome the attachment to our afflictions or whether our afflictions will overpower and obscure our wisdom. To be able to make a clear choice, we need stability of mind, and our heart needs to be open. This makes it possible to make a choice free of affliction, and instead to maintain a wholesome attitude benefiting others and ourselves. The mirror-like wisdom quality within each of us allows everything we encounter to touch our heart and mind. It also allows us to keep these encounters free of the distortions caused by our afflictions and thus to have our heart and mind touched by the deeper and undistorted reality. And it protects us from getting carried away by pain and suffering or by the intensity of our habitual needs.

The second quality needed to support discriminating wisdom is the wisdom of equality. Wisdom of equality refers to our capacity to embrace reality with acceptance and compassion. When we have fully realized the wisdom of equality, we will naturally leave things as they are without effort, without having a need to change, improve, or control them. What is this equality? Why do we see it as wisdom? Wisdom of equality puts an end to the judgment inherent in dualistic thinking. It helps us overcome the conditioned response of judging that divides our mind. When the mind is divided, it loses its strength, and we lose the capacity to make clear decisions. When our mind lingers in the confusion of this divided state, consciously or unconsciously, things start falling apart.

The divided mind does not have a strong reference point to give it stability and trust. It dwells in the realm of doubt, fear, and chaos that arises from our projected self-judgment and is further destabilized by internal insecurities and external distractions. The wisdom of equality helps us to not be misguided by these insecurities and external distractions but to keep an open mind and skillfully discern how to benefit all sentient beings, including ourselves. It leads us to realize that we are not separate but that we are all one. This realization of oneness is the basic nature of compassionate beings. Following the path of equality allows us to treat everyone equally. It allows us to see through our wisdom eye, to feel with the heart of compassionate acceptance, and to think with a mind of all-pervasive openness.

CHAPTER 9

MEDITATION

Meditation is the process of observing the stream of our consciousness with mindful and open attention in order to create a calm and peaceful space within ourselves, so that our emotional instability and mental distraction can come to rest. Meditation is the application of the mind and sense fields in order to retain stability of mind and stability of emotions. We are maintaining a stable, open presence that holds sensual impressions in its space of awareness without being carried away, yet also without excluding anything. Meditation is also the process of developing a harmonious connection between the physical, emotional, and mental dimensions of our being. Meditation methods found in the Bön practices of Sutra, Tantra, and Dzogchen have a common intention. This is to help ourselves and others be free from the cyclic continuum of suffering.

Many of us want to know how we can use our meditation practice to really transform our lives from suffering and to move toward the direction of awakening. We do this with the deep wish to change the habitual conditioning that our afflictions are based upon. Our acceptance and recognition of our afflictions and their causes is key to actualizing the essence of the practice of meditation. It is not the number of mantras that we accumulate, or the hours spent sitting on the cushion. If we come to our practice with the sincere heartfelt wish to transform ourselves, to become more compassionate, even a short meditation session can change us deeply.

First of all we need to be really clear about why we are meditating. Otherwise, our meditation can be a trap rather than the doorway to liberation. We might think, for example, that we are doing something good for others and for ourselves or that we are saving all beings, while in fact we might be feeding our delusions. To avoid this possible trap, we need to become aware of and accept the parts of ourselves that might be less wholesome and less conscious than our motivation to do good and benefit others. Accepting all of ourselves, including our weaknesses and delusions, is often difficult. In fact, we may be practicing because we are actually looking for a way to leave our weaknesses behind. However, in order to be able to touch into the awakened mind that is beyond the grasp of suffering, we need to first befriend our suffering and pain and its nature. We need to look deeply into the relationship between our practice and the afflictions which cause our suffering. We may think that we are working on transforming our suffering, but in actuality we may be pushing away the parts of ourselves that we do not like. This is very restricting to the birth of the awakened mind in us.

GETTING USED TO MEDITATION

We have a saying in Bön: "gom pa mayin goms pa yin." This means: "It is not about meditation; what it is about is to become familiar." We become familiar with the nature of ourselves, both wholesome and unwholesome, and thus with the nature of reality. We become familiar with the stream of our consciousness and with its function, and we develop a quality of heart and mind that is able to perceive unfamiliar perceptions or situations without reacting with ignorance. We become more and more familiar with the qualities of our true nature: compassion, love, joy, equanimity, and innate purity. When we develop these qualities of heart and mind, our suffering is reduced. This will bring ease and joy into our lives and increase our physical, mental, and emotional well-being.

Why is familiarity so essential to the practice of meditation? Once I was flying from Atlanta to Albuquerque. I was seated in the middle seat, and the window seat next to me was open. A man appeared who looked beautiful and also a bit unusual. He had a shaved head and his whole arm glowed with the fire of many colorful tattoos that went all the way up from his hand to his shoulder. He pointed to the window seat and said, "I am sitting there." As I looked at him pointing with his hand I saw that he had a mala, a string of prayer beads,* on his wrist. That very moment, when I saw his mala, it changed my whole perception. How did that happen? It happened because I am familiar with seeing someone with a mala. Seeing his mala brought a feeling of ease into my mind and body. It made me feel that we were connected. Often when we discover something familiar in a stranger, the sense of him or her being a stranger to us is dissolved, and we have a feeling of connection instead of a sense of alienation or judgment. I could have made the stranger in the airplane the object of my judgment based on fear and unfamiliarity. But just having seen the mala on his hand changed my whole being and protected me from entering into a state of habit-driven judgment.

---

* A mala typically consists of 108 beads.

When we take time away from external influences to be quietly by ourselves, we get to know ourselves in an intimate way. We become familiar with ourselves. We become familiar with our stream of consciousness and the way that our emotions are produced. We become familiar with the way that we live our lives. We become familiar with the process that happens in us when we become agitated, and with our weaknesses and strengths. We become familiar with what it is to be sitting with strength in the face of depression. We become familiar with our ego, with our attachment to our physical body, our afflicted emotions, and our fear of death. And we become familiar with our addiction to our fear.

Through becoming familiar with what causes us pain and suffering, we will be able to see what is subtly exhausting and killing us internally through jealousy, anger, fear, sadness, or loneliness. Through this process of becoming familiar, we can develop the heart and mind to know what to renounce and what to accept. In this way we become familiar with our innate healing wisdom and with our own potential Intimate Mind. We become familiar with the Buddha within. The Buddha said that you are your own best friend and your own worst enemy. The practice of meditation can give us the strength to see these qualities of friend and foe within ourselves. Our gentle acceptance of these different qualities within can help us to become aware of and observe the stream of our consciousness and how it contributes to our physical, mental, and emotional distractions and instability. Meditation can help us to calm our mind.

Once I went to visit a friend who lived on a beautiful ranch where scientists were working on the protection of an endangered sea turtle species. That evening, all of us were invited for dinner. While we were enjoying our dinner, one of the scientists said, "We as scientists produce data and information on the basis of facts and observations. This is what we provide by the end of our day. What do you produce by the end of your day as a religious practitioner or meditator?" That was a question of awakening for me at that moment. What is it that takes birth in my mind and my whole being by the end of the day? It is calmness. By the end of my day, I feel calmness, ease, and joy.

In our lives, there is calmness and joy on the one hand, and anger, depression, sadness, desire-attachment, and impulsive pursuit on the other. There is much chaotic energy whirling around in our mind and body. This is why we need to learn to harmonize the movement of our energy with the calmness or stability of mind that we cultivate in our meditation. Sometimes we may think that meditation will take care of all our problems just by generating enough calmness. This is not possible, though, unless we learn how to integrate this calm state of mind with the chaotic movement of our energy. Just sitting by itself does not bring ease and eternal joy and take care of our emotional insecurities, although it helps us to settle the monkey mind that constantly moves from here to there. The calming of the mind is not realization in itself; it is just a first and preliminary step. Our actual liberation from the cyclic continuum of suffering is only possible if we become familiar with our afflictions and learn to use our calmness and our concentration to reduce the chaotic movement of these afflicted energies.

Meditation has the power to familiarize us with the qualities of our true nature, our potential of Intimate Mind. In the Bön Buddhist tradition, we have a set of meditation practices called preliminary practices. We do these practices to turn our mind toward our innate compassion, wisdom, purity, and equanimity. The preliminary practices are designed to gradually bring the mind back to its true nature. If we have a notion to build a garden, before we can do that, we have the vision of what the garden will look like; and this vision will affect us, the place, and our actions. But that is not enough. This is just an idea, a concept. We have to actualize it. How do we do this? We gather the seeds, and we research how to cultivate them, what ingredients are needed and how to take care of the young plants. And still this is not enough. We need to till the ground, then put the seeds in, mix them up, and take care of them day by day. Still, after all this care, we don't know whether the seeds are going to grow. If they don't grow at all, how will we feel?

The preliminary practices create the foundation for our gradual recognition of our true nature. Through our steady, dedicated practice we become accustomed to its qualities, which means that we become familiar with generosity, with the mind of compassion and awakening, and ultimately with our pure nature. The practice imprints itself onto mind and body in the form of qualities such as patience, openness, and acceptance. A beautiful gift of meditation practice is that it keeps us connected with the miracle of each moment. It allows us to see the beauty and the shadow of every moment and how these small things affect us. It helps us to release our attachment to preconceived results. It brings us closer to the reality of life by allowing us to use both suffering and happiness as part of our practice toward the realization of awakened heart and mind.

THE INTERRELATIONSHIP OF SUCCESSIVE STAGES OF MEDITATION

In the first stage of meditation—Calm Abiding—we unify the mind with its object of attention. The practice of Calm Abiding is a powerful practice to help us develop a quality of mind that can hold focus and presence. With this practice eventually we will manifest the mind that cuts through all delusions, the mind that will enable us to see the other side of the shore. Through the practice of Calm Abiding we become familiar with the wandering of the mind without grasping onto mental formations. This is carried out through the concentration practice of mindful attention.

The second stage of meditation—Insight Meditation—is about stabilizing the mindfulness that we are developing during the first stage. Here we begin to direct our awareness to the unification of concentration on one hand and our feelings and emotions on the other. The intention of our practice at this stage is to realize Self-awareness. This is also referred to as Insight Meditation. At this point, our concentration practice becomes undivided. The one who concentrates, the act of concentrating, and the object of concentration become one.

The third stage of meditation is to realize Open Presence. Here, our feelings, emotions and self-awareness itself are being unified with emptiness.

POSTURE

We begin our practice of meditation with the proper body posture that allows mind and body to unify. The flow of our energy in the form of the circulation of our blood or the circulation of our breath links body and mind to each other. When body and mind become one, we experience a sense of relaxation. But when the body moves, the mind will move also. This is because of the intimate connection between body and mind. We could say that the body is a vessel that contains the mind. The mind is used to reacting whenever the body moves or is affected. It is therefore essential to settle the body first, and then work toward settling the mind.

In the traditional Bön path of meditation, the essential aspects of the body posture are to sit cross-legged, to keep the spine straight, to gaze in a line that extends directly and very slightly downward from the tip of the nose, to sit up with the chest open, and to rest the hands on the lap with the tips of the two hands touching, and the two thumbs touching the base of the respective ring finger. This five-point posture of meditation trains the mind to maintain spontaneous awareness. Whether we are aware of the five aspects of the posture depends on the subtle subconscious aspects of the mind. If we really maintain our body posture, this means that we are equally distributing the mind, not only on the object of our attention, but also to all aspects of the posture. This strengthens the quality of awareness. If we maintain this quality of acute awareness every time we meditate, we become it, and we will have it wherever we are. That is the gift of meditation.

Yet, the most essential aspect of body posture is to find a posture with which we can feel at home. When there is a sense of alienation or resistance, it will be difficult to go beyond this; it might actually take us in the direction of aversion. We are practicing meditation to nourish our lives and to reduce our suffering. And we are practicing to help others. We are not practicing to add more pain and suffering, even if it is just in form of a back pain or knee pain. Therefore, in our meditation practice we do not do anything that hurts ourselves and hence has a negative effect on others as well. Rather, we carry out our meditation in a very skillful way that allows mind and body to settle and to feel at home. Through this we can reach into the essence of transformation.

Some of us are very new to the practice of meditation. It is essential to take it easy and to proceed slowly. I remember one retreat of eight days of sitting meditation. Every day we began our practice at 5:30 in the morning and ended the last practice session at 10 at night, with just a short break in between. I liked it very much, just being with myself in a very intimate way. But there

were many other participants who had never done such meditation practice before. The instructions were to attend the meditation sessions no matter what condition we were in. This was a
situation where it was easy to become overwhelmed not only by
the discomfort of actual body-pains due to the lack of experience and practice, but further to become overwhelmed by our ego
which may pressure us with feelings of shame, guilt, and the fear
of being weak. We want to be strong in front of others although
our back and knees are in great pain. And we want to sit on the
cushion just like others. We think that if we sit on a chair, this
will make others think that we are not strong enough, or we think
that this will make our practice less fruitful. We force ourselves
to engage in an action that goes against the capacity of our bod-
ies and our minds. When there is pain, there is duality, and when
there is duality, the nature of the mind is divided and disturbed.
To engage in this conflicted manner will only corrupt our moral-
ity. It is very important to take a posture that is comfortable to
us—particularly in the beginning. Then we can slowly adapt it, as
we get used to it. It does not matter whether we sit on a chair or
on a cushion, in the full lotus or half lotus. The important thing
is that we keep our body firm and grounded, so that the mind can
take refuge in the firmness of our posture.

THE FIRST STAGE OF MEDITATION:
CALM ABIDING

Once we are well settled into the firmness of our body posture,
the next essential aspect of Calm Abiding meditation is our object
of attention and the development of concentration. We use an object of meditation in order to become familiar with the wandering
of our mind. We can choose any object on which we can put our

attention so that the mind has a place to rest. It can be of great support if we choose an object that we feel connected with. This will make it easier for us to pay attention, and we do not have to use a lot of effort to develop concentration. Also it is important not to change the object of our meditation too often, but rather to stay in touch with just one object at the developing stage. In many meditation traditions, people use their breath as the object of their concentration. This is very effective and beautiful. Our breath is always with us, whether we are aware of it or not. We are deeply familiar with the process and nature of our breath, and we know how important it is to our very lives. It is also very helpful that our breath is something we do not have to create by any means or method. It is already there with us from birth.

We enter into Calm Abiding meditation through the development of concentration.

First Stage of Concentration

In the first stage of concentration, we place our attention on the object of our meditation. Our ability to rest the mind on one object at a time helps us minimize the constant wandering of our mind and the resulting arousal of thoughts. This practice of single pointed attention, together with distinguishing between the object of the mind and the mind's wandering, helps us to make progress in our practice. The sign of progress in using an object of concentration is that the mind is stable, and that there are fewer distractions by external objects or afflicted thoughts. Through this practice of focused attention we enter into a state of mind that connects us with the calmness that is born from our practice of attention and the withdrawal of the mind from wandering. We experience joy because we enter into a state of being that is free from the distress caused by the process of distraction and the arising of discursive thoughts.

Second Stage of Concentration

In the second stage of concentration we no longer need to discriminate and evaluate the thoughts that arise as much as before. We have become increasingly familiar with the nature of our thoughts and with the process of their arising and their influence on the arising of our emotions. This gives us stability and confidence in the focused state of the mind, and we gradually become able to just let be whatever arises, without grasping onto the peaceful state of our experience, or rejecting the arising thoughts. Our perception is always supported by causes, in that it is defined by some concrete idea or concept. Thus, any experience created by the mind is conditioned and impermanent. This realization is important in order to be able to live fully in the moment. Our state of mind is now characterized by increased focus, internal clarity, and a quality of concentration that is pure and free of discrimination, evaluation, and rejection of thoughts. We enter into a state that is calm and even, without grasping, judging, discriminating, and rejecting.

Third Stage of Concentration

This very even and calm state is the third stage of concentration. Here, the mind has become familiar with the body posture and with the object of our attention in an intimate way. We begin to experience our mind coming home as it rests on the union of our body, mind, and the object of our attention. This stage is characterized by equanimity. Because of our single-pointedness and internal clarity, the mind is fully engaged. It is completely absorbed into the object of our attention, and we remain in equanimity, mindfulness, and alertness. We develop a quality of mind that is free from grasping and craving, and we enter into the state of Calm Abiding. Our unconscious grasping loses its nature and becomes awareness. This awareness is the manifestation of boundless consciousness.

How do we do this? Do not follow after discursive thoughts, and do not reject them. Do not create discursive thoughts by inviting past experiences of any nature or by anticipating future plans. Simply stay in the state of being aware in the present moment. Here, quite naturally, the mind itself will become the object of our concentration. In doing this, do not fall into a state of unconsciousness, but leave everything as it is with a strong presence of awareness. Do not try to fix or change anything. Just abide in this state of awareness for as long as possible. Even if it is just for a few seconds, we will experience the great gift of this practice.

MEDITATION AND THE OBSTACLES OF THE FOUR MARAS

There will be moments when the mind tends to wander under the influence of internal or external distractions. We might think that we are in a state of just being aware or focused, but later we realize that we disconnected from the object of our attention quite a while ago. If we resist and start to struggle with that experience of constant distraction, it will cause us a great deal of mental and physical exhaustion and more distraction. This subtle unconscious exhaustion can lead us to a point where we feel agitated or tired. When we are in this state, our Maras can take advantage of our vulnerability, and we might see ourselves as failures and feel discouraged. This will hinder our practice.

In Bön Buddhism, afflictions and delusions within ourselves that distract us from our awakened nature are called "Maras." Maras are not external forces, but parts of us. In fact, our Maras draw their power from the separation of our present state and our pure nature created by the conditioned mind. As long as we operate out of this separation, we cannot develop true confidence in our practice and in ourselves. If we are not confident, we may feel the need to constantly defend ourselves against anything that might expose our weaknesses and against the differing views and ideals of others. Then we will not be able to benefit fully from our practice.

If we can accept our weaknesses with an open mind, our fears and judgments toward ourselves and others drop away. It is this openness and acceptance that makes it possible for us to learn. This motivation is not just something that we need for the practice; it already is the practice. We cannot have a dualistic motivation and expect that it will carry us into non-duality. We cannot learn to truly love others without fear and judgment if our motivation and practice are based on an attitude of not accepting ourselves. Judgment will not bring forth love. If we can learn to familiarize ourselves with our conditioning, it becomes possible to use everything that we encounter for our practice.

One of the most beautiful gifts of mind training meditation is that when the mind is distracted or has become carried away by one of our Maras, we can use that very moment as an opportunity to cultivate a quality of awareness that is characterized by self-compassion, forgiveness, patience, and determination. If we can do this, it means that our meditation is developing. It is moving toward its essence. Self-compassion and forgiveness will put an end to our thoughts of blame and provide a space for confidence. This helps us to bring the mind back in a gentle way rather than forcing it. On the other hand, patience and determination will keep us on the path of practice with strength and dignity.

Mara of Ego

The first Mara is the Mara of ego. During our meditation, we may become aware of our ego grasping in a very subtle way. We may grasp at our constructed sense of who we are, our self-identity as we perceive it or would like it. If we fail to recognize this, it will confuse our perceptions and disturb us. It leads us to develop a sense of self-identity that dominates our experience. Or we may experience absence of thoughts during our meditation and grasp this as the ultimate realization. It is our notion of an existing self that develops both our attachment to the ego concept and to the experience of no thought.

How can we work with this Mara through our meditation practice? We can clear our mind from holding on to a particular faith, belief, or view. We can practice not holding on to an expected outcome, but rather following the path of meditation practice with a quality of acceptance and determination. We keep watering the seed that we have placed, without letting any idea or preconceived notion of outcome distract us from our path. The most helpful practice to open the doorway of liberation for this Mara is the practice of loving kindness. When we have true loving kindness, we include all beings and their happiness and suffering in our practice of meditation. Thus, whenever we meditate, the first few minutes we connect with our motivation to help all beings—including ourselves—to be happy and free from suffering. Then we go back to our actual meditation, whether this is watching the breath or whether it is the visualization of a deity.

Mara of the Five Aggregates

The second Mara is the Mara of the five aggregates. This Mara is our attachment to our physical body and to the five aggregates of form, feelings, mental formations such as views or judgment, perceptions, and consciousness as a self. Our grasping is a result of our perception of objects as pleasant or unpleasant, right or wrong, and our dualistic reaction of liking or disliking.

When caught in this dualistic thinking, we develop a strong positive attachment for what we perceive to be right or pleasant, and a strong negative aversion-attachment toward what we regard as wrong or unpleasant. This Mara causes distraction through our attachment to form, feelings, perception, and consciousness, and it prevents us from going beyond what we are attached to. In this way it sows the seed of conditioning. Being attached to one particular thing and to the notion of like and dislike narrows our mind and heart, and prevents us from realizing our true nature of equanimity.

In order to work with the Mara of the five aggregates, we need to become aware of the lack of a separate inherent existence of any one thing, and we need to become aware of the interdependent nature of all beings. The most important antidote to the Mara of the five aggregates is the practice of the Ten Perfections*. The positive qualities of mind that we develop through practicing the Ten Perfections enable us to let go of our attachment to this body and to form, feelings, and perception. They enable us to not attach ourselves negatively to our enemies or positively to our friends, but to realize that we are not separate from either. Our happiness and our suffering depend on the interdependent nature of existence. Once we recognize that we are all interdependent, we will truly experience happiness, and we will see our happiness in others' happiness, and others' suffering in ourselves. If we can develop this genuine feeling, we will abide in the wisdom of equanimity and embody the essence of non-separateness. The realization of non-separateness frees us from the grasp of the Mara of the five aggregates.

---

* The Ten Perfections are the practice of generosity, the moral conduct of our three doors of body, speech and mind, patience, effort, concentration, power, compassion, aspirational prayers and dedication, skillful means, and discriminating awareness.

Mara of Afflicted Emotions

The third Mara is the Mara of afflicted emotions. This Mara keeps us attached to our afflicted self-centered emotions. It acts as the main cause of our emotional distraction and instability. The meditation practice of concentration can subdue this Mara. While we are meditating, our distraction may manifest as a sense of drowsiness, dullness, or agitation. If we experience any of this, we do not force ourselves to carry on the practice of meditation. If we are feeling drowsy, our energy or strength is weak. For our meditation practice to be productive, we need to rest and renew our energy. We might do some walking meditation or chanting. Sometimes we are exhausted after a long day of work and nights in which we cannot sleep well. It is not healthy to do meditation in that state of tiredness and low energy.

When we experience dullness and our object of meditation or visualization is not clear, we may try to force ourselves in order to get more clarity. We may think that doing meditation will reduce our stress. However, if we force too much in such a situation, it might damage the proper functioning of our brain. A simple helpful approach when we feel dullness in our meditation is to do our practice in shorter sessions.

Sometimes, we may experience feelings of agitation during the practice of meditation. We may try to concentrate or apply more focus, but find ourselves easily disturbed by the intensity of our emotions, the arising of thoughts, or by external objects. If we feel too agitated, it is best to stop our meditation for the time being. Anything we do against the natural flow of our capacity might cause pain and suffering in our lives and may, in fact, lead to psychosis. This is because of the pressure that we put on our brain. In the meditation practice of concentration, the mind is forced to control its own functions along with the chaos of our emotions. On the one hand, we are trying to control the mind and its mental formations. On the other, we are using the mind itself to carry out this activity of controlling itself. It is necessary to be gentle and open when we do our practice of meditation. It is important to receive proper meditation instructions from someone with extensive meditation experience and to have someone who can advise us on our practice also at later stages. If we are not too agitated, we can learn to work with our arising thoughts. In the meditation practice of concentration, we do not engage with the arising afflicted thoughts, and we do not create a new thought that has the same nature. We calmly abide in the state that is free from the constant distraction of thoughts.

There is a tendency to activate our Mara of attachment if we hold on to a blissful state that we experience in Calm Abiding meditation. The state we are experiencing imprints itself onto the mind, and we develop desire-attachment toward it. We develop a concentration of grasping. The next time we do meditation practice, if we do not get to that same state of experience, we feel that something is wrong, and we suffer. Holding on with the power of grasping, we always want more—and we become addicted. Meditation practice is intended to break through this and any other kind of attachment. We need to let our concentration be one with our awareness—just noticing, without expecting or grasping onto what we are experiencing.

Grasping concentration is always directed toward desire-attachment, whereas meditation is directed toward awareness. If our concentration is one with awareness, rather than one with grasping, our experience of whatever happens can flow freely without obstructions and without creating suffering. If our mind grasps onto the blissful state of our meditation experience, we cannot go beyond the grasping of concentration, and our meditation won't be able to affect us positively and change our conditioning.

Mara of Mortality

The fourth Mara is the Mara of mortality. This Mara is our attachment to the continued preservation of our ego or our habitual conditioning, and the fear of its death and total annihilation. To get to understand this Mara intimately and be able to overcome it, we need to practice the acceptance of the truth of mortality, or the impermanent nature of all compounded phenomena. Practicing the acceptance of the truth of mortality cuts the root of our ego. In the Bön tradition, we have a very beautiful and powerful practice called *Khandro Sang Chod.* "Chod" means to cut off. What is cut off in this practice is our grasping of the ego and our habits, and our attachment to its continuation. Our holding on to the self feeds the Mara of mortality and imprisons us in the cyclic continuum of suffering.

When we practice meditation, we may have an experience of our true nature. Due to the Mara of mortality there is a tendency to project that this experience will stay the same forever, and we begin to hold on to it. However, everything changes. As the experience we have during our practice begins to change, our projection and expectation of its permanence will destroy the benefit of our practice. We can work with this Mara through the practice of Open Presence.

THE SECOND STAGE OF MEDITATION:
SELF-AWARENESS

Over time, the progressive stability of the mind becomes awareness that keeps our energy in its natural flow. This is Self-awareness. Self-awareness is the fourth stage of concentration, and its realization is the second stage of meditation. In the fourth stage of concentration, we go beyond the blissful and joyful state of our mind. There is no grasping onto the bliss and pleasurable sensation of feelings, or onto sensational feelings of resistance or aversion toward any pain that we may be experiencing. Rather we abide in the pure equanimity of neither pleasure nor pain, and in mindfulness. This is the wholesome concentration relied upon by myriad practices of body, speech, and mind of the compassionate being.

Our meditation may proceed to the realization of Self-awareness once the quality of our concentration has become quite deep. During our concentration practice, our effort is needed to bring our attention to a single point. Our practice requires diligence, effort, and the qualities of determination and persistence. Our concentration is not permanent. It is temporary. It can be broken or interrupted by our habitual conditioning, by habitual reactions, or by external objects at any moment. In the practice of Self-awareness, we have an object of attention that is being observed, we have an observer who is doing the observing, and we have the act of observing or concentrating. However, as long as these three remain separate, our practice remains limited, and Self-awareness cannot be realized. This is because we grasp onto the state of being focused on the object of meditation and onto the corresponding sensational experience. This sensational experience may be a blissful state of relaxation. It may be a sense of seeing, of touch, of the movement of energy within us, or an experience of qualities such as love, compassion, or peace.

When we are focused on one thing, we might not be able to perceive beyond that what is happening around us, because we are so absorbed in the act of focusing on the object of our attention. When we are aware, the mind is equally distributed. When everything is brought into the field of our awareness, the conditions for distraction are greatly reduced. If the mind is focusing without this quality of awareness, a sensational experience such as a sound caused by an external object that is stronger than our focus on our object of concentration will cause us to be distracted. In this case, instead of remaining focused on our actual object of concentration, the sound becomes the object of our attention without our being aware of this shift. If we are self-aware, we are aware of such subtle internal activities of our consciousness and of what is happening around us externally without the distraction of judgment, aversion, or blame.

We have a story of two dancing skeletons, "The legend of Cittipati." Once there was a yogic couple that was well known for their accomplishment of concentration practice. One day while they were meditating, they got lost in deep absorption of concentration. A thief came by and cut off their heads and took all of their possessions. They did not notice that their heads had been cut off. Later they vowed to become wrathful enemies of the thief in their next lives in the form of dancing skeletons to scare away the thief. This story reflects the importance of awareness in the practice of concentration. Concentration brings the mind onto the object of its attention, but awareness understands the nature of the object that we are observing or experiencing. When concentration and awareness unify, insight is born. And this insight gives us a myriad of choices and freedom.

Once our concentration becomes deep enough to sustain itself without forceful effort, its nature becomes unconditional. At that point, we are not just paying attention to one object as a focal point, but rather we bring into the field of awareness the whole of our being, external objects, internal sensations, or experiences of the movement of the energy within us. We observe the rising and dissolving of our thoughts and the movement of energy in our body. And we observe the interdependent nature of mind and body and how it gives rise to emotional feeling. We must do our best to clear all internal and external preoccupations to allow ourselves to become one with the object of our awareness so that we are really able to observe the subtleties of the interaction of body and mind.

THE THIRD STAGE OF MEDITATION:
OPEN PRESENCE

When everything is brought into the field of awareness, the concentration of equanimity is born. This is where the third stage of meditation, Open Presence, comes into being. In this stage, the concentration of the mind becomes objectless. We are doing meditation without an object of concentration, and we do not hold on to anything. When there is freedom from grasping, we are actualizing the vast nature of reality. This is the realization of spontaneous concentration or Self-awareness that further allows us to gain insight into innate awareness, the nature of the mind, which is unconditional and free from all afflictions. Self-awareness is like the sun that has the capacity of illuminating its surroundings but that also illuminates itself. It is self-luminous. Innate awareness, on the other hand, is the innate potential of the mind, the clarity that is the unification of emptiness and awareness.

In the practice of Self-awareness, we direct our attention toward the observer himself or herself to experience the innate quality of the nature of the mind. When we turn our attention toward the mind in the form of the observer, we go beyond the grasping onto our meditation experience of sensational relaxation, and carry out our inner journey of self-inquiry so that we can experience the true nature of our being. When we release our grasp on the particular taste of our experience, this allows the quality of Self-awareness to unify with emptiness. This is Open Presence.

The true nature of our being is pure and not afflicted. Through the act of merely observing without reacting in the presence of awareness we clear the afflictions produced by our intellect. This is because the power of spontaneous concentration together with awareness brings the stream of our consciousness and its activities into a state of stability and equanimity. When the mind is in a state of equanimity, the activities of our consciousness that give rise to afflictions come to an end. For instance, if our mind passes through our eyes at the moment when we look at a flower, our eyes, the mind, and the flower will become one. At that moment, our consciousness is in a state of equanimity. It is free of the afflictions of intellect such as judgment, resistance, or aversion, and its experience retains its nature without distraction. When the meditation becomes spontaneous, the arising of wisdom becomes possible.

Self-awareness is the unbroken form of concentration. When the subject, object, and the process carried out by the subject become one, the totality of oneness is experienced. This results in self-realization and the state of experiencing great bliss. When all our afflictions, the chaos of our emotions, and the wandering of our minds come to rest, that is self-realization. Self-realization abides in the heart of Open Presence. At this point, we embody great equanimity, and bliss arises because we are completely free from distraction and from mental formations, at least for the time being.

To practice Self-awareness and realize Open Presence, we need a stable mind. Without the genuine practice of stabilizing our minds as a fundamental base, our practice of Insight Meditation or meditation of Self-awareness would be like a flower without a root embedded into the earth. It would be like a flower that is in a beautiful vase with water in it. The water can keep the flower alive for a while, but in the absence of its root, its life cannot last long.

CHAPTER 10

OPEN PRESENCE—

THE MIRACLE OF EACH MOMENT

The ability to leave things
as they are
and to be intimate with each thing
in every moment
is the essence of Open Presence.
Within the spontaneity of Open Presence
the unique qualities of our innate nature
manifest at every moment.

We all have an inherent potential to become a Buddha. However, we are often not aware of this. Not being aware of our potential, we are unable to manifest it. We empower our conditioned nature rather than our Buddha nature. Because of our deep-seated conditioning, we cannot recognize the truth or the reality we encounter in our life. In the practice of Open Presence, we face each moment as it is without fear and without judgment. To do this we need a loving and compassionate heart and the wisdom of understanding. These two qualities enable us to perceive things as they are. By turning away from things as they are, we create a wall between reality and the nature of the mind. This is one of the major reasons for the suffering in our life.

The essence of Open Presence is clarity, the unification of emptiness (or the interdependent nature of all things) and awareness. When we unify emptiness and awareness, we do not hold on to our concept or understanding of emptiness nor to awareness. When we hold on to awareness, it no longer remains awareness; instead, we grasp the perception we are having at that moment and it begins to dominate our mind. Perception is impermanent and not truly substantial. When we are free from holding on to awareness, we are able to recognize this.

On the other hand, our perception is not just empty. This is the clarity aspect of Open Presence. Open Presence is about recognizing the unified nature of emptiness and awareness. Emptiness and awareness are not separate; they are co-arising, or inter-being. Sometimes we live in the relative world and practice for the world of the absolute. We live on this earth, and pray for heaven. Being open and present helps us to not fall into the dualistic extremes of relative versus absolute or of heaven versus earth. To the practice of Open Presence, these two are not separate. They are one. Can we realize the absolute nature within the relative, so that we do not wander in search of the absolute truth, riding the surf board of the relative?

ASPECTS OF OPEN PRESENCE

We begin practicing Open Presence by becoming familiar with both the nature of openness and the nature of presence. Open Presence has these two inherent aspects that become one through our practice. Openness reveals the nature of emptiness. Presence reveals the nature of awareness. Through our understanding of these two qualities we can bring them into the path of our practice as one. Without this understanding our practice becomes just an idea, a philosophy. It will come and go without any stability or fruition. But if we actualize its meaning and integrate it with our experience of the world outside and inside of us, we manifest its essence. We live in the present moment. We do not mistake our concept or understanding of emptiness as actual emptiness itself, nor do we hold on to awareness. Otherwise our concept or judgment will dominate the mind and distance it from its true nature. When we are free from the grasping imposed by conditioning, we make it possible to experience reality as it is. When we practice Open Presence, we manifest this unified nature of emptiness and awareness within the continuum of each moment.

For instance, how can we manifest the qualities of openness and presence through the simple practice of listening? Openness is the ability to provide space for another person to speak by giving non-fear and by providing space within ourselves that allows us to hear without judgment or disagreement. Openness is not limited to the listener only. When the listener is open to the one who is speaking, that very act of openness gives the speaker a space to be more open as well.

When we are present, we are able to recognize what is needed in each moment. We know we do not have to take care of, respond to, or fix everything all the time. Often our rational mind thinks that we have to correct, respond to, or give advice to others. Yet, sometimes it is so valuable just to bear witness and leave things as they are so that they can unfold in their own way without our intervention. Leaving things as they are is the essence of Open Presence, and it is one of the greatest challenges on the path of a compassionate being. Over time, the practice of Open Presence empowers us to develop this capacity. When we practice Open Presence, we witness every situation without being distracted by external objects and demands or by our internal conditioning.

When I came to the United States, many of my new friends told me that people here in the West do not listen to each other very much. When I heard one of my friends saying this, my first thought was to ask her, "Do you listen to others?"

She stopped for a moment and said gently, "Oh, that is interesting..."

My feeling is that if I do not have the heart, mind, or time to listen to you, how could I possibly expect you to listen to me? This example brings to mind the importance of mutuality, the nature of interdependence. If you listen to the other, even if they do not listen to you, he or she will feel the gift and blessing of your presence. That will definitely bring a change in the quality of their being.

Sometimes we encounter a situation where someone is not listening to us. We may start blaming the other for not listening to us or we may personalize that person's lack of attention and feel rejected or hurt, and thus judge ourselves. This is one of the basic obstacles for the Intimate Mind caused by unmet psycho-emotional needs that may be unconscious. We lose contact with our innate wisdom, our capacity to be non-judgmental, and with our innate qualities of acceptance, forgiveness, love, and compassion. We need to ask ourselves: Would it be possible to accept the other person as they are in that moment with genuine compassion? When we are able to do this, we connect with our basic human nature of goodness. Would it be possible that behaving skillfully with openness and love would inspire the other person to listen in turn to us? I think it is possible.

Awareness enables us to provide a firm space of equanimity for the mind so that we can see and hear without judgment. Then we can understand what the other person needs and what we need. We or the other person may not be in the position to answer each other's needs. But we can do our best to remain compassionate, loving, and forgiving. We can do our best to embody the quality of mirror-like wisdom so that we can understand the other's situation without arousing our own afflictive conditioning. If we are able to provide what the other person needs and what we ourselves need, we can stop the suffering resulting from the situation. Even if we are not able to do that, simply being in touch with the quality of awareness helps us to reduce the causal conditions for suffering.

When we bring both openness and presence, both awareness and the knowledge of emptiness to our afflictions and our state of mind in each moment, we make it possible to recognize that these very emotional states are not separate from the nature of the mind:

> *When you realize*
> *there is no separation*
> *between patience, anger,*
> *sadness, or depression*
> *and the nature of your mind,*
> *that is the essence of liberation.* *

Seeing any emotion as negative energy is ignorance. And following that energy through our negative attitude leads to great delusion. The practice of Open Presence gives us clarity that is powerful enough to recognize that whatever emotion we experience, be it anger, depression, fear or joy, is not separate from the true nature of the mind. Emotions of any nature arise as a result of karmic causes. But if we do not interfere with them, they will also dissolve. If we are able to recognize this and do not attach ourselves to an emotion that arises, the intensity of that emotion will be much less distracting and less destructive. This recognition is wisdom. It gives us the strength to leave things as they are, which reduces our subconscious attachment to the emotion and the unnecessary pain and suffering that is related to it. We may suffer because we question why the situation to which we are reacting is happening. We may suffer because we are working against the emotions with which we

---

* Adapted from the Zhang Zhung Nyen Gyud Bön Dzogchen teachings.

respond and are trying to get rid of them. We create suffering by separating our emotions from the true nature of our mind.

If we have the heart and mind to recognize that whatever emotion we experience is not separate from the true nature of the mind, we are accepting our emotion. We become aware of what we are feeling right now, and we stop right there. We don't allow that emotion to take over our life. We make peace with whatever we are feeling. If we cannot do that, the energy of the emotion may manifest in a different form. If we feel disappointed, for instance, this may give rise to anger. If we feel angry, it may give rise to hatred or to depression. This is unnecessary. If we can accept what we are feeling, we manifest the essence of self-liberation. We leave each thing as it is.

Why is it important to leave things as they are? It is important because by nature everything is self-arising, self-luminous, and self-dissolving. Everything comes, and it goes. It does not stay forever. But this is only possible if we allow it to manifest its nature. If we hold on to it, it could also take a lifetime to dissolve.

Clarity of mind recognizes the nonseparateness of our emotions from the true nature of the mind. This recognition is liberation because we become free from emotions that act as obstacles to the functioning of our stream of consciousness from our true nature. If we are able to accept our emotions as not separate from the nature of the mind, this will allow us to touch our healing wisdom. Our healing wisdom is our primordial potential to heal ourselves and to free ourselves from suffering. We all have this potential. If we have anger, we also have love and compassion. Emptiness reveals the truth that nothing lasts forever. Awareness points us toward this truth and allows us to experience it. Their unification—clarity—gives us the strength to live with the constant demands of our everyday lives with ease and joy and to allow our every experience to self-liberate into its own nature.

MANIFESTING OPEN PRESENCE
IN EVERY MOMENT

We approach our life with many expectations based on our insecurity or pride, uneasy past experiences, or projections about the future. These expectations limit our openness, our ability to be aware, and to accept each situation as it unfolds. Many situations we encounter may be unexpected and we may not be prepared for them. As a consequence, we are not fully aware of them as they happen, and of their effect on us. It is this lack of awareness along with the instability of our mind that makes us react with a state of distress or shock, and that renders us vulnerable to separating ourselves from the situation.

We encounter many situations in our everyday lives that make us feel hurt or disturbed. It is very important to reflect on our state of being in that moment with awareness so that we can recognize what we are feeling. This recognition itself gives us the strength to look into how our feelings of that moment have come into being. Sometimes we are so disturbed by an incident that we lose control of ourselves and disconnect from the wisdom of our mind and the compassion of our heart. The situation that made us feel hurt might already be over and gone. If we let it go, impermanence can work its miracle, and our suffering will cease. What usually happens, though, is that we make things worse for ourselves by holding on to the situation through our reaction of blame, self-justification, or guilt. We do this because we want to feel safe and protected. This instinct toward protection can be so strong that it completely overshadows the presence of healing wisdom in us.

Usually when a situation affects us in this way, we do not notice it. Sometimes we notice that a situation has affected us because we find that our mind continues to return to it, and to become caught up in the subtle negative emotions that arose in us in response to the situation. Because we are inclined not to notice such reactions, we may think that they do not matter much. But the totality of these small negative reactions and the unconscious habits they create in us are what separates us from our true nature.

Lack of awareness will strengthen the afflictions that prevent us from seeing reality as it is. When mind and body are governed by self-centeredness or by emotions such as fear and self-protection, we lose control of our state of mind and our actions. Awareness enables us to see what is going on with clarity. Awareness in the form of penetrative wisdom cuts through the afflictive emotions that are present in us in the process of reacting. It protects us from unnecessary reactions based on our insecure conditioning, such as reaching out with anger or other afflictive emotions, or with unwise compassion. Unwise compassion is, for example, when we see another's suffering and invite pain into our own lives by being hard on ourselves in response. In such a case, our compassion is not supported by wisdom. It is mixed with our attachment and insecurities rather than with wisdom. Then our feelings for the other cannot become true compassion but instead become the expression of our insecure conditioning.

The practice of Open Presence teaches us how we are distracted by ten thousand things every day, every hour, and every moment. Many things, such as external objects we perceive through our sense fields, constantly influence us physically, emotionally, and mentally. Some of these are shocking and disturbing, some are pleasurable, and some are joyful. The tendency of our conditioned human nature is that we are only attracted to something that is beautiful, comfortable, and that we feel familiar with. But if there is something that makes us feel uneasy, we react differently. This can be the way somebody behaves, or something that somebody is saying to us that we cannot relate to or that is opposed to our feelings. Or it could be an unpleasant sight, smell, taste, or touch. When we encounter an uncomfortable perception through our sense fields, including the mind, this distresses us. The practice of Open Presence prepares us to live with such moments without distress or fear. We have the innate potential to liberate ourselves from the suffering of those moments.

At the heart of Open Presence is the question of how we can respond to every situation we encounter in our life from the true nature of the mind, rather than with a deluded or afflicted state of mind. The practice of Open Presence empowers us to leave things as they are. When we leave things as they are, we provide space for them to manifest the ever-changing quality of what they are. Due to our conditioning, we tend to interrupt everything before it can manifest its true nature. It is that very interruption that obscures our wisdom and our compassionate heart from reaching out to others and reaching inward to ourselves.

We might wonder what our wisdom and compassion have to do with the practice of leaving things as they are. In the practice of Open Presence, our wisdom manifests in the form of clarity. Clarity allows us to be aware of the situation without distraction. And our compassion keeps us stable and allows us to reach out with equanimity so that we are at ease, no matter how things manifest. If wisdom and compassion are present together, we can make a decision at that very moment, without being governed by our preferences.

OPEN PRESENCE AND FORGIVENESS

My deep wish and prayer is that every being on this earth may find the strength of heart and mind to forgive each other when we encounter another's unskillful actions. If we don't forgive the other with love and compassion, we let the energy of that situation affect our whole being. This will lead to our feeling hurt, rejected, or angry. By not being able to forgive the other or the situation, we may empower the situation to turn into something much bigger. This will cause ourselves and the other person further pain. If we have the quality of strength to forgive, we are not inviting pain and suffering into our life.

Sometimes it is not easy to forgive because we are so affected by our feeling hurt about something that has happened. How do we integrate clarity into these situations, so that our disturbed feelings can self-liberate? How can we have the quality of heart and mind to be able to stay calm and in touch with our compassionate heart in the midst of the pain we may be feeling? We cannot cultivate this heart and mind of strength and forgiveness by turning away from the situation. We cultivate it by facing the situation in a very honest, loving, and compassionate way.

Developing the capacity to do so will take time. This is because of our strong habitual conditioning that has been accumulated over a long period of time. We may have grown up under the influence of constant reactivity to painful situations. We may be inclined to think that there is no way to respond differently and to be free from the need to feel affected and to resist the situation. But there is a way to be free if we look within.

First we need to have compassion. Usually what happens when somebody is angry with us is that we become inundated with our fears, our feelings of insecurity, or our hurt feelings, and we let these reactions dominate the whole of our being. This is where Open Presence reminds us to be aware and not to react right away. This may be difficult, but it is possible. We do this with the support of reaching inward to our compassion and mindfulness and stopping for a moment before we reach out. Compassion and mindfulness will help us not to blame either ourselves or the other person. They give us the strength to look deeply into the situation so that we can see the causes of the other person's feelings and the causes of our response.

Being aware means, first, to notice the situation fully. If our friend is angry with us, we notice that by bringing it into the field of our awareness. When we notice a situation with awareness, we have a natural potential and instinct for how to respond in a skillful way. If our friend is angry with us, we can ask ourselves whether we really love her or him. If we really love our friend, we can let our clarity help us unify with our feeling of love at that moment. We can draw strength from our love to be able to forgive or accept our friend or the situation. This is what the Bön teachings refer to as unconditional love and compassion. If we are not able to do that, we are letting the energy of our friend affect us. We are inviting his or her chaotic energy to dilute and distract our wholeness. On the other hand, if we approach the situation with the presence of clarity, our unconditional love for our friend can manifest and express itself in how we respond. It will manifest whatever is necessary at that moment of our life.

Sometimes our unconscious self-centeredness pressures us to react. We feel that the other person is not respecting us. We can ask ourselves: Do we really have to be respected? What difference does it really make, whether we are respected or not? Of course we have to respect each other and not take advantage of each other, but our attachment to our identity, our personality, our character, our role, and our responsibility in this world pressures us to react when someone is not respecting us in the way that we expect. Often we feel that if we do not defend ourselves, we will not be able to feel good enough. Or we may feel that we are the one who is to blame for the situation. This attitude of constant self-protection subtly invades and corrupts the nature of our mind, preventing us from forgiving and causing us suffering.

It is our ignorance in the form of ego or self-centeredness that comes in the way of our forgiveness and of our own and others' happiness. Our self-centeredness does not allow us to understand where the other person is coming from or to accept her or his situation with compassion. It does not allow us to see who the other really is. If we can really see and accept where the other is coming from and what he or she is feeling, that is forgiveness. The gift of forgiveness is to be able to transform oneself into the other person, so that we see through the other's eyes. It provides the strength to understand and respect what the other person is seeing, thinking, and feeling, and it allows us to listen through her or his ears. We are able to speak through the other's mind and to feel from his or her heart.

If this is not possible, then we can at least try to provide a firm space for the truth of the situation to unfold by itself without being hindered by our reaction. When we do this, the gift of impermanence, of evolution and completion, can reveal itself spontaneously. We are giving space to the situation through our forgiveness and respect for the other, through our deep listening, and through the quality of bearing witness to the other and to ourselves. If you and I do this practice, together we can do much to lessen the intensity of unnecessary pain and suffering in our own lives and in this world.

In this process we need stability and clarity of mind. Stability helps us witness the state of our mind, our feelings, and the situation. It enables us to give space to our mind to respond in a skillful way without becoming unnecessarily disturbed or a victim of our conditioning. If our mind is clear, there will be fewer chances for misunderstanding and becoming impaired by the delusion of ignorance. When clarity and stability are both present, our energy becomes calm. This enables us to respond with the quality of Open Presence.

CHAPTER 11

RECOGNIZING THE PRESCIOUSNESS

OF OUR LIVING LIFE

Loving our life
and taking responsibility
for happiness in every situation
is the essence of the Intimate Mind.

THE PRECIOUSNESS OF HUMAN EXISTENCE

Part of the practice of the Intimate Mind is to shed light onto our life, to understand the preciousness of our life, and to appreciate how difficult it is to have the opportunity to be born in this human form. In the Bön tradition of Tibet, to be born in human form is the best condition compared to the other five possibilities: the hell realm, the hungry ghost realm, the animal realm, the demigod realm, and the god realm. The concept of hell is found in many spiritual traditions. In the Bön tradition it is believed that one is born in the hell realm as a result of karmic conditioning accumulated within the continuum of our existence. The major causes for being born in hell are our anger and the unwholesome deeds of our body, speech, and mind that are based on anger.

In many traditions the hell realm is understood as a metaphoric representation of continuous suffering. We may think that we are now in human form and will not go to hell. Or we may think that hell does not exist. My personal belief is that the hell realm exists in this very life, within the continuum of our existence. Different spiritual traditions constantly remind us of the fact that the hell realm exists. They do not do this because they intend to scare us or to make our lives miserable, but because they want to direct us toward our true nature. The preciousness of being in human form is that we can work toward freeing ourselves from endless suffering. We can learn and become familiar with the cyclic continuum of suffering through our direct experience. One of the great gifts of being a human being is that we are gifted with a heart and mind that understand love and compassion for ourselves and others. Also, we feel and understand the pain and suffering of others. Having witnessed our own suffering and pain, we wish for all other beings to be free of suffering. We can choose to refrain from any action of our body, speech, and mind that will bring suffering and pain into our lives and the lives of others.

In the hungry ghost realm one constantly suffers from hunger and thirst. We can take this as a metaphor for suffering, yet the truth is that suffering of this nature does exist in our lives. Just like hungry ghosts, we are never satisfied with what we have. Instead of being content with our life, we constantly engage in accumulating more and more things. In this process we make friends with greed and desire-attachment. It is our very act of greed and attachment that serves as the main condition for the creation of the hungry ghost realm. As a human being we also have the choice to not fall into such a realm. But under the strong influence of greed and desire-attachment all our perceptions are controlled by these emotions, and we are not able to think beyond their grasp. We are so obsessed by the conditioning of greed and desire-attachment that we lose connection to our inherent capacity to love and to be compassionate. When there is no compassion or love, we cannot think about others in a positive way. All we can think of is how to make ourselves happy, even if we have to destroy someone else in order to fulfill our own desire. Working toward our happiness is genuine and important, but bringing unhappiness into another's life in the attempt to achieve our own happiness will not bring us true happiness. What is even more important is to realize the conditioning and suffering that we are attaching to ourselves in every instant of our lives through greed and desire-attachment. If we realize the power that greed and desire-attachment have over us, we can make the choice to free ourselves from their grasp and to not bring suffering to others or ourselves as a result of that conditioning.

In the Bön tradition, we say that beings are born into the god realm as a karmic consequence of having accumulated good karma and having performed wholesome activities in their past lives. In the god realm, beings have everything they could want. They have the capacity to fulfill all their needs, expectations, desires, and dreams. It is the place where your every wish can be fulfilled without any hindrance or obstacle. Beings in the god realm enjoy perfect health and very long lives.

Why is it then, that life in the human realm is more suited to the path of compassionate beings than life in the god realm? Once we are in a state where everything we desire is freely available, we may lose connection with our natural appreciation for the joys of life and for the causes and conditions that have contributed to their manifestation. Even as ordinary beings, sometimes we are so lost in the realm of abundance in our lives that we no longer recognize love, compassion, generosity, joy, happiness, and the sense of helping others. For instance, when we are in love with someone, there is a tendency to become so used to the love that it becomes a conditioning that prevents us from perceiving and accepting anything else. Our friend has become the source of our love and joy. If our friend has some difficulties, we find it difficult to relate to her because we are not familiar with her problems. In that moment when she needs our help, our conditioning prevents us from accepting and loving her unconditionally. We may feel that our trust and our ability to rely on our friend are gone. When this happens, we fall back into Samsara, and we experience suffering.

This is even truer for beings in the god realms. As beings in the god realms come closer to the end of their lives, their recollection resurfaces and takes them back to the earlier stages of their lives. They then begin to feel remorse that they have not done anything good and have instead gotten lost in the midst of the abundance in their lives. They have a feeling that now they are going to die and lose everything. They have become used to having everything without the need to worry about anything. The consequence of becoming used to this is that the abundance itself becomes a conditioning. In the end, this conditioning reveals its true nature: the feeling of attachment and regret. This very sense of regret and the attachment to what they are losing creates a wrong view in the form of discouragement. The simple thought that they have not done anything truly good could change everything and turn them toward the aspiration of a compassionate being. However, this does not usually happen. The habitual conditioning of attachment that has been accumulated over time is so strong that discouragement manifests instead. So, after a life in the god realms, beings tend to fall back into the cyclic continuum, and Samsara continues.

I would like to connect the notion of the god realm to those beings who are gifted with resources of all kinds. In this world there are many fortunate beings who have everything, and there are others who struggle every moment of their lives to survive. In Tibetan culture, one would say that to have a very fortunate life is due to an individual's karma, or that it happens because of wholesome deeds in a past life. It is also believed that if one performs virtuous deeds in this life, one will have a better and prosperous life in a future birth. Given my limited knowledge of life after death, I would not go that far. However, if we carry out wholesome activities, they will bring us happiness in this very life.

I am very grateful to those fortunate beings who are in the position of helping others with their skill, knowledge, wealth, or wisdom. They have the power and capacity to help many beings with their gifts. Often, when we are blessed in this way, we become absorbed in this identity and use it to achieve fame and power and to accumulate more material goods, rather than to accumulate merit through helping others. Using what we have solely to fulfill our own wishes is an unwise use of our gifts, our knowledge, and our specialties. People who lack in resources, skill and knowledge are in need of you. You are the true compassionate being in your own capacity who can bring a light into the lives of many beings who are in need, and who are in search of that particular light you have.

In the Bön tradition, part of our daily practice is to do prayer and offerings. Our offerings are not just limited to food, jewels, or wealth. We offer incense, candlelight, water, and musical sound. This is because we believe that there are many beings who live beyond what we can see with our naked eyes. There are some beings who rely only on the spirit or soul and who are liberated through sound, smell, touch, taste, sight, or through lights. We can see some of that even in ourselves. Sometimes listening to chanting or to music brings our heart and mind together and takes us into a space where we feel completely calm, at ease, and awakened. Even when we perceive the fragrance of a camellia, it may pause our busy minds for a moment. It cleanses all our fatigue and stress and connects us with the moment. Clearly, the resources and knowledge we have are not just limited to particular objects or words. I believe each individual has an ultimate resource to benefit others and her or himself.

LOVING OUR LIFE

Loving our life
is the gift of an open heart,
and unconditional love
is the wisdom of the Intimate Mind.

Hearing and thinking about the situation in the hell realm, the hungry ghost realm, the demigod realm, and the god realms can give us a different perspective on our lives. We have to know our own situation and where we are situated in our lives as human beings. Then, appreciation for the immense gift of our life can arise in us. Even if you and I were to consider ourselves among the poorest beings on this earth, we have the ultimate resources to benefit and liberate ourselves and other beings to the greatest level of joy and ease, and moreover to freedom from all afflictions. We have the potential of Buddhahood.

If we cannot recognize this gift within, there is a possibility we will become a burden to this earth. If we break our heart by believing our circumstances are not enough or by feeling unworthy, we break our confidence in our own inherent potential. This is judgment. There is a tendency to lose our stability and confidence through our obsessive judgment of ourselves. It is important to remember that we don't know what we are contributing. In actuality, every moment we are affecting, touching, moving, and helping many beings. This happens in a very natural and unconditional way.

Is it necessary for us to notice the many ways in which we are affecting others or the ways in which we are changing someone's life? More essential is to stay in touch with our good motivation not to harm anybody, including ourselves. To have this motivation toward ourselves plays a crucial role. The moment we say something critical toward ourselves, we lack self-forgiveness and self-understanding and make ourselves vulnerable to chaotic influences that can weaken us. Self-forgiveness gives us the strength to grow and to mature. It gives us the strength to connect with other beings, and with the situations we encounter in our life in ways that will be mutually enriching. Also, it frees us from our attachment to difficult past experiences.

It is through loving, respecting, and being honest with ourselves that we find the strength in us to forgive others. From the very natural experience of being kind to ourselves, we can bring that quality into someone else's life. Every single animal, human being, and living thing on this earth, including ourselves, is looking for something: Forgiveness when something goes wrong, compassion when one is suffering, love when one is in despair, peace when there is chaos, water when there is thirst, food when there is hunger, warmth when there is cold, kindness when there is hatred, strength and confidence when we begin to freeze with fear.

It can be easier to forgive others because we can see through their needs, and the situation allows us to connect with our love, compassion and kindness. It is often difficult to forgive ourselves. In this case, the one who forgives and the one who is forgiven are the same. When we are in a situation where we are negatively affected by our own actions, our mind becomes dominated with our feelings about the incident that has just happened. To forgive ourselves, we accept what we have done, and we accept our state of being. This is not going to happen if we stay in the state of being affected. From that state of mind there is no possibility of forgiving. However, our mind has both the potential of delusion and the innate potential of Buddhahood. If we manifest only the deluded, affected part of our mind, we will not be able to forgive. We need to activate the unaffected, nonjudgmental nature of our mind by separating our mind from its contact with the state of being affected by a situation. This unaffected nature of our mind has the innate potential of self-compassion and forgiveness.

Self-forgiveness is so important because kindness and compassion for others have to come through ourselves. Kindness and compassion for others are not possible if we do not have the capacity to have that same kindness, compassion, and forgiveness for ourselves. The ability to forgive others is rooted in our own direct experience of how we can transform our suffering. For instance, when someone criticizes us, we have the tendency to react and to put ourselves into an unhealthy state of being. We resist what we hear because of our lack of forgiveness and openness. Our resistance generates a feeling of pain in us, and that feeling of pain leads us into suffering. Our suffering may even become a depression that remains with us for a longer period of time. We need to learn from our experience how to transform and liberate ourselves from becoming the victim of this unnecessary suffering. If we can do this, we are loving our life and realizing our true nature.

To love our life, we have to recognize the gift of our potential and the causes of the cyclic continuum of suffering. We must understand the law of cause and effect and believe in its essence. Can we have the courage and love to open our heart and mind to see the pain and suffering of this world and the suffering of our own lives with true clarity of mind and true openness of heart? If we can do this, we will be able to face the suffering of others and ourselves, and our insecurity, fear, and confusion, without letting them take away our strength or obscure our wisdom. Then we can do our best to free others and ourselves from the suffering of cyclic existence. The practice that we do for our own liberation and for that of others is not just to gain peace of mind or to feel good. The essence of this practice is love and compassion, and our motivation is to help others and ourselves in the deepest way possible. We practice so that we do not engage in any kind of physical, mental, or emotional state of our being that obscures the reality of all phenomena. This obscuration is the cause of our engaging in unwholesome actions of our body, speech, and mind. Not letting these obscurations afflict us is the practice of liberation.

If we love our life, we also have a close familiarity with the impermanent nature of all phenomena, including all beings. Every single thing is characterized by the universal truth of impermanence. Nothing lasts forever as it is. From the smallest elementary particle to the giant stars, everything is going through a continuous process of change. Looking into our lives, we also go through many changes we are not aware of. Even if we understand the reality of change and are aware of this truth, we still tend to hold on to something, thinking that it will keep us happy, healthy, or peaceful. We know things change all the time, but there is something in us that holds us back, that doesn't allow us to really accept that nothing stays the same. Being familiar with the impermanent nature of all phenomena means we remember our mortality and recognize and accept that some day all of us will die. We keep this truth in our mind and develop a quality of mind and heart that reminds us all the time of the gift of this life and to appreciate it, no matter what situation we are in.

When we love our life, we do our best to be fully present in whatever we are doing, from gardening to meditation to office work. Being fully with what we are doing involves letting go of our expectations, while at the same time being aware of the external and internal consequences of our actions. We can begin to do this by looking into our motivation for our actions. Often, when we are interested in an activity, we have some kind of expectation, and this expectation prevents us from letting our mind unify with what we are doing. Also we may be doing our work because we have deadlines or a schedule to follow. We may have future plans related to our work and the planned accomplishment. We may physically carry out an activity such as watering a plant, but our mind is talking with our friend in the restaurant and having a glass of wine. Later, when we are having the glass of wine with our friend, our mind is again somewhere else with another activity. This distraction, our expectations, plans, and the pressure that we put on ourselves create constant interruption that gets in the way of each experience and the act of fully engaging with it and becoming one with what we are doing. When we are not fully present, we cannot experience the essence of each moment:

When the mind unifies
with what we are doing,
free of expectation
and judgment,
a very practical sense of joy
and ease can manifest.

Sometimes our response to circumstances we are not happy about prevents us from loving our life fully. We look for ways to change our circumstances or to get away from them. Once we have successfully changed our circumstances, we may find that our suffering continues or begins in a new place in a similar form. In fact, taking action to change our circumstances may have prevented us from recognizing that suffering exists in our mind and is not an intrinsic part of difficult circumstances. Circumstances that are not easy to love and accept are part of life. Yet, the reason we suffer is because we do not accept how we respond to our circumstances, and we do not acknowledge our own potential. Can we find the heart and mind to love ourselves in difficult situations, with our fear, our stress, and our impatience? The ability to do this holds the potential for great healing and for reconnecting with our natural wisdom and strength. These are the very qualities we need when we face difficulties.

Clearing our mind from distraction is another aspect of loving our life. Distraction occurs because we develop dislike of specific conditions in our lives and specific aspects of ourselves, be it our appearance, our level of education, or our physical abilities. These are the distractions that do not allow us to love our lives and ourselves. Such judgment creates a split in us. We begin to discriminate between things we like and things we don't like. We begin to judge ourselves and feel constantly in competition with others. Distraction may also arise when we do not accept an incident that has occurred in our lives, or if we do not accept ongoing conditions. We may feel this way about a major illness or accident, a loved one's death, or about a handicapped or sick relative we have to take care of. Often we do not recognize that we have entered a situation with a lot of expectations. When things do not happen the way we expect, this can cause us immense suffering.

This suffering is not just about the situation. Often it is our judgment or a feeling of shame that makes the situation so painful for us. Our expectations and our self-judgment can exhaust us and make us sick.

When someone in our life is handicapped or sick, it is natural to wish that he or she may have a better life. It is very good to have this wish for others, but if that wish becomes the cause of our pain, it is not healthy. Developing the heart and mind of acceptance can be very difficult in such a situation. We need to really understand why we keep talking about acceptance here. If I accept from the bottom of my heart that my son is mentally ill, then that is just what is. I do not need to let it affect my heart and soul, neither through my own expectations nor the way other people talk about him. That is acceptance. Doing this frees us from much of the suffering that results from our fear of people's judgment and from our own expectations. This is a beautiful way to love our life and to live fully in each moment. When we love our life, we do our best to reduce our pain and suffering. If we do this, and if we continue to follow in this direction, we are taking responsibility for the happiness of our life and the transformation of suffering. If we can do so in each moment, this is the essence of the Intimate Mind.

THE GIFT OF FRIENDSHIP

One of the great gifts that make life beautiful is the gift of friendship. Being aware of the support that we receive from our friends can give us the strength to connect with the heart and mind of gratitude. Our life is a journey made of many different components. One of the most intriguing of these is that we meet other beings and build relationships, be they of joy or of suffering. However, there is a natural truth that when we meet someone, there will eventually be a separation. The story of life is one of union and separation. We tend to have concepts and ideas about this that cause us to have a different response to these two facets of life. When we unite with someone through friendship and love, we see this as positive. But when we face the truth of separation, that is difficult and we cannot let go.

My grandmother used to say that love between two beings is like the grass and the dewdrop. Their relationship has the mystery both of oneness and of two distinct identities. When the dewdrop falls to the ground, their relationship continues without interruption, as the dewdrop now nourishes the grass. But our perception tends to be one of separation and pain. This is because we create a habitual conditioning through meeting and uniting with others, and this conditioning makes it hard to let go. The union with another being has become the source of our joy. But this union is always followed by the shadow that is separation. If we are willing to accept this truth, it will make a huge difference in our lives. We will be able to live in the moment with both union and separation.

In my own life I value immensely the importance of friendship. In this journey of living life we meet so many beings. Some remain as a memory in our minds, some live in our hearts, and others disappear. The beings who touch our heart contribute to the nourishment of our life in a way that is beyond expression. They live with us in each step that we take. This gift appears in different forms of love, strength, and hope. Friendship and love are not just limited to the people we are close to or to human beings. Friendship and love are the qualities of support that each individual on this earth receives from and offers to others, making our lives more complete, whether that other is a human being, a squirrel, a flower, water, or air.

Love in the form of acceptance, generosity, and gratitude is the true essence of awakening. We can practice love in every moment of our lives. What does it mean to love in the form of acceptance, generosity, and gratitude? Love that is based on our expectations and needs and seeks to fulfill them or love that is based on desire-attachment is not truly unconditional love. As the practice of a compassionate being, love is not self-oriented, but seeks to make the other happy. The generous aspect of love is that we not only expect love and understanding from the other, but also offer these to him or her. We look into her or his needs, letting go of our conditioning and expectations about how things ought to be. Instead we give as much space as we can to who the other is. We give space to what they need, we give them respect, and we listen. Loving in this way is one of the most powerful ways in which we can support someone's development of confidence, strength, and capacity to connect with their own loving heart. If in a relationship two people approach each other with this kind of love, the nature of their relationship will be one of joy and happiness, and there will be less suffering and pain.

When we truly love someone, we cannot hold back, and giving becomes natural. As we give, our whole being relaxes and fills with happiness and ease. When we love someone in this way, this love has the element of connection. When we feel connected, we are open. This very connectedness and openness generates a quality of generosity in our heart and mind. We should not underestimate the power of our love, service, and friendship, and the positive contributions that these have in another's life. We all connect with many beings throughout our lives and receive their care as friends, parents, children or grandchildren, students or teachers, or husbands or wives or lovers. The loving care we receive strengthens our capacity to connect with our own true nature of love. As we touch others with our true nature of love, the gift of love and care others have given us actually reaches out to many more beings than just ourselves. In the same way, the love that we give to others can, through them, touch many beings. Our love and friendship become part of the inspiration for others to enter the path of a compassionate being.

Love is intimately connected with gratitude. The connection we make with anything through true love makes us and the other happy and allows us to connect with our true nature. As we experience this love, we feel gratitude. When we feel love for a person, a situation, or an object, that person or situation helps us to connect with ourselves, with the part of our heart and mind that makes us feel the depth of our love. Can we have a heart and mind to appreciate the presence of those we love in the form of gratitude? When we feel gratitude, we accept and acknowledge the contributions of that person, object, or situation. The feeling of gratitude is one of selflessness. When we truly feel grateful for the love we are being offered, we will wish to do the same for others, so we can become the inspiration for others to connect with their own loving nature. That is true giving.

Sometimes there is a tendency to take the gift of love and friendship for granted and to lose touch with the gift of our gratitude for the love we are experiencing. If we walk the path of a compassionate being, we can do a simple practice of consciously bringing our loved ones and their gifts to our mind as often as we can. This helps us focus more on the qualities of service and gratitude and on our capacity to love unconditionally. This practice clears our mind and heart and turns our heart toward unconditional love.

We can accumulate material possessions, and we can earn wealth, but we cannot earn the true love of friendship. Unconditional love is the inherent nature of sentient beings. Where there is love, there is awakening of our heart and mind, and there will be trust. Trust and patience are the strengths of a true friendship. They help us understand and accept the weaknesses, pain, and suffering of others, and help us forgive others with our love and compassion. On the path of compassionate beings we truly connect with others and form friendships based on love and compassion, free from the expectation of gain and fame. Any relationship that is built on the foundation of expectations and needs will remain weak, and sooner or later will collapse. But if the relationship is built on the foundations of love and trust, it will continuously grow in strength and meaning. The practice of the Intimate Mind is to become friends with all beings and to love them equally. That is the greatest gift we can give to ourselves.

> *Nights are not old nor are the days*
> *they come and they go*
> *yet the coming and going of day and night*
> *whispers into my ear to wake up*
> *so that you and I can dance*
> *with the miracle of each moment*
> *in this journey of living life*
> *before we return.*

SUGGESTED FURTHER READINGS

Latri Nyima Dakpa Rinpoche
Opening the Door to Bön.
Snow Lion Publications, 2005.

Dalai Lama
An Open Heart: Practicing Compassion in Everyday Life.
Back Bay Books, 2002.

Thich Nhat Hanh
The Heart of the Buddha's Teaching.
Three Rivers Press, 1999.

Dilgo Khyentse Rinpoche
The Heart Treasure of the Enlightened Ones.
Shambhala, 1993.

Dzongsar Khyentse Rinpoche
What Makes You Not a Buddhist.
Shambhala, 2008.

Lopon Tenzin Namdak
Bonpo Dzogchen Teachings.
Vajra Publications, 2006.

Chögyam Trungpa Rinpoche
The Heart of the Buddha.
Shambhala, 1991.

Tenzin Wangyal Rinpoche
Wonders of the Natural Mind.
Snow Lion Publications, 2000.

ACKNOWLEDGMENTS

My heartfelt gratitude to my family: my grandparents the late Kalu Lama, the late Dane Lama, the late Tashi Lhundrup Lama, the late Samtenma Lama and Karsangma Lama, my uncle the late Kangri Lama, my parents Phuntsog and Serzangmu Lama, my parents-in-law Brigitte and Wolf Grossmann, my aunts Nangsal, the late Dolma Chokyi and Serzangmu Lama, as well as Tsering Yeshe, Tenzin Norbu, Tenzin Paljor, Norbu Sangpo, Cho Dolma, Kundol, Tashi Cheozum, Lumo Tso, Yung Drung, Bhadur, and Kangzum Lama.

I am deeply grateful to my teachers His Holiness 33rd Menri Trizin Lungtok Tenpa'i Nyima Rinpoche, Geshe Chongtul Rinpoche, Yongdzin Tenzin Namdak Rinpoche, and Menri Ponlob Thinley Nyima Rinpoche. I want to thank all the Bön teachers who have inspired my path, supported my work, and shared the gift of friendship with me, including the 7th Kundol Namkha Wangyal Rinpoche, Dongrig Lama, Tsewang Ngodrub Lama, and Khenpo Tenzin Dargye.

I want to express my deep gratitude to Roshi Joan Halifax for her love, support and inspiration and for introducing me to the West. My deep thanks to my friend Morgonn Bryant who inspired and encouraged me to begin writing this book. I am grateful to Judy and Barry Wagner, James Bradbury, Sandia Douglas, and Unzan Pfennig for their love and continuous support.

I would like to thank Lowell Britson for his support, skill and dedication in making this book and Olmo Ling Publications become possible. My gratitude to Margaret Bashaar, Dianna Eden, Judith Jaynes, Jenny Lee, Mary Lynear, Renee Rabache, and Ursula Teuter for reading the first draft of the manuscript and offering valuable comments. I would like to thank Jean Grace for editing the final version of the manuscript. I deeply appreciate her sensitivity and skill with the English language.

I am very grateful for the support of my friends, including: Lisa Abbot, Annette Adams, Jaccqui Barr, Keith Barrett, Kate Bazis, Adrienne

Block, Kathleen Bogacz, Dewitt Bolden, Emily Bopp, Kate Breithaupt, Louise Brooks, Annie Brown, Terry Browning, Philine Bunte and Björn Grossmann, David Cantor, John Carleton, Marilyn Carpenter, Mai Cashion, Sandy Chan, Laura Chapman, Judith Chase, Carol Cirigliano, Debby Conway and family, Marjo Curgus, Andrea D'Amato, Sarah Dawson, Jim Delbianco, Debra Denker, Nelson Denman, LuAnne DePons, Nyima Dondup, Joan Downing, Verona Fonte, Christine Frechard, Junko Fujisue and Paul Wells, Sherry Gage, Simone Garrigues, Rose Gordon, Carol Greco, Nyima Samdup Gurung, Lama Gyurme, Heidi Harding, Miyo Harumi, Alexis Higginbotham, Pillar Hood and family, Anzan Steven Hyde, Marie Jackson, Elizabeth Jacobson, Ekta and Mia Khandro Jansen, Milo Jarvis, Margaret and Chris Jasielski, Andrew Kaiser, Tom Kalson, Sandhya Karki, Jean Kotchision, Bob Labobgah, Chhewang N. Lama, Jigme Lama, Mangol Lama, Phunzok Lama, Sanga Lama, Surendra Lama and family, Yangjor and Babita Lama, Yangze Lama, Joe Lazarra, Eric Little, Jessie Litven, Kichung Lizee, Katinka Locascio, Jennifer Lowe, Paco Lugovina, Timon Malloy, Laura and Bob Marin, Felicia Marohn, Kris McCann, Sue Motz, Eileen and John Nadzam, Daiken Nelson, Josh Nicholson, Kimmerly Novosel, Mayumi Oda, Roshi Pat Enkyo O'Hara, Beatrice and Manny Oquendo, Gary Pasternak, Erin Peepels and Eric Mason, Nancy and Stan Perelman, Joel Pirchesky, Trish Podgorski, Charlene Reader, Clare Rhoades, Neela Richardson, William Rock, Katherine Romero, Susan Russell, Noemi Santana, Andy Sethi, Mark Shefsiek and family, Henry Shukman, Sandra Smiley, Libba and Jon Spiegel, Christina Stadlbauer, Elizabeth Stow, Tek Tamang and family, Tova and Joel Tarr, Tsering Tashi, Gary Terner, Archie Tew, Gretta Thomas, Maria VanDusen, Mihnea Vasilescu, Mary Viola, Susan and Bill Wagner, Pauline Weddle, Courtney and Ryan Weikle-Mills, Birte and Jan Weinbecker, Janaki Welch, Lori Wertz, Jean Wilkins, Joel Wilson, My Wiseman and River Gibeaut, Nancy Wood, Charles Woods, and Mingyur Youdon. I also want to thank my friends who grew up with me in Menri Monastery and many other friends.

I would like to thank my beloved wife Iris Grossmann for her love and support, for continuously helping me with my writing projects and for supporting my vision of Olmo Ling.

Olmo Ling is a non-profit organization dedicated to preserving the teachings of the ancient Tibetan Bön tradition and making them available and accessible in the West. Based in Pittsburgh, Pennsylvania, Olmo Ling Bön Buddhist Center offers a program of practice and studies in the three Bön paths of liberation: Sutra, Tantra and Dzogchen.

In order to preserve the wisdom of the Bön tradition, Olmo Ling is dedicated to publishing Bön teachings, including new commentary texts and translations of essential Bön practices. Through the Olmo Ling Project on Death and Dying, Olmo Ling offers training and practice in healing, compassionate care and spiritual support for the dying.

If you would like more information about the teachings of Tempa Dukte Lama or the activities of the Olmo Ling Bön Buddhist Center, please visit us at:

Olmo Ling Bön Buddhist Center
1101 Greenfield Avenue
Pittsburgh, PA 15217

tel: 412-904-1112
fax: 412-421-1472

email: bon@olmoling.org
www.olmoling.org